McCoy, Jim,
The last place you look
: a contrarian's guide t
[2016]
33305236981837
la   01/10/17

THE
LAST PLACE
YOU LOOK

A CONTRARIAN'S GUIDE

TO DATING AND

FINDING LOVE

JIM McCOY

The Last Place You Look:
A Contrarian's Guide to Dating and Finding Love

by Jim McCoy

Copyright © 2016 Jim McCoy. All rights reserved.
Printed in the United States of America.

ISBN: 978-0-9972294

To NJW, without whom NFW.

CONTENTS

FOREWORD

A couple of things inspired me to write this book. First, I'm a life coach, and I like helping people figure out how to be happier. When they come to see me, many of my clients are alone and not entirely happy about it. It's very satisfying to help them change that, and while I love to do that one person at a time, I decided I could reach many more people by writing a book.

Another thing that inspired me was that I had been there myself in the not-so-distant past, and I set to work doing something about it. It took me a while to understand what I was doing, but eventually I felt like I had it pretty well figured out. After three and a half years of dating I found Nancy, the woman who would become my wife.

To prepare for this book, I've collected anecdotes from all sorts of people who've been out there in the dating trenches. Young, old, men, women, straight, gay, bi—these experiences are universal. I'd like to use their stories and my own to help you learn from our mistakes and successes.

INTRODUCTION

Love is the best part of being human.

Love matters, and it matters to you. The trick is finding it, and the usual way of finding it is through dating.

Lots of us are not so thrilled about dating. We hate the uncertainty, the pressure, the confusion, the awkward conversation, the dashed hopes, the difficulty, the discouragement, the tedium. We only like dating when it works the way it's supposed to.

So let's make it work the way it's supposed to.

As you read this book, you'll answer three questions for yourself that will help with that process:

- *Why* do I want to find a partner?

- *What* exactly am I hoping to find?

- *How* am I ever going to do it?

You want somebody in your life, somebody you don't have now. And you want to know how to find that person, but you're frustrated by dating. It's my hope that by the time you finish reading this book, you'll not only feel less frustrated, but you'll be actively looking forward to the process, you'll like yourself and your life, and you'll be enjoying all of the connections that you're making. Then you'll find your partner, in the last place you look.

If you're hoping for secrets on how to pick someone up, or how to be irresistible, this is probably the wrong book for you. Being skilled at seduction can actually work against you as you try to find a great lover. Rather than connecting with someone in an authentic way, you might manipulate them into liking you, and you'll potentially get entangled in something that is doomed to fail from the start. You might get some fun and some temporary companionship out of the deal, and that could be a good thing in the short term, but it's probably not going to do much for your long-term happiness.

Stop worrying about seduction. And please, please, please stop worrying about dating. A problem that many people have as they're looking for love is that they invest too much emotion in every date. Too much hope. Too much fear. Too much effort. And if it doesn't work out, too much disappointment. Before they know it, they dread dating, sometimes to the point of avoidance.

When you go out with someone, or when you're just having a conversation, you're not on a job interview, and neither is the person talking to you. *In all probability, the person in front of you will not be your future spouse.* So why get stressed? You're simply meeting someone. Getting to know them a little. Don't worry about the date: it's not important. Just see how you relate to the person you're with.

Maybe they'll become part of your life in some way. They might turn into a great friend, they might introduce you to somebody, or maybe they'll teach you something interesting. Who knows? You're making a connection, and if you make enough connections, one of them might turn into something great. And that's it. Once you understand that, and really live it, you'll be on your way. You'll not only have a better chance of finding the right person, you'll have a better time doing it.

It might not be as hard as you think.

Several years ago, I found myself single again in midlife, and I made a decision. I decided that I wanted a woman in my life—a *good* woman—in order to have the best life I could. I'd already been working on putting together a decent life without a partner, but I knew that wasn't going to be enough for me in the long run. I wanted more. So I went to work, with my eyes open. I went to work meeting with women anyway I could.

I knew it wasn't inevitable that I'd find the right person, but I resolved to be focused and diligent about trying. I connected with lots of women in lots of ways—sometimes for no more than a cup of coffee, sometimes for dinner, sometimes conventionally, sometimes unconventionally—over the course of three and a half years.

Somewhere along the line, I became aware that I'd been out with more than a few women, and being something of a numbers geek, I was curious about how many. So I decided to keep track. I combed through my memory, I checked my email, and I came up with something like 22 different women at the time, and I began counting. 22 became 30, and 30 became 40, and next thing I knew, I'd gone out in some way with 68 different women. The last one, number 69, was Nancy Werlin, who became my wife. She has improved my life in so many ways, and she's been more than I'd even been hoping for. My life, which a few years earlier had seemed pretty rough, is now really, really good.

You can have that, too. Here's how.

A QUICK NOTE ON PRONOUNS:

This is an unusual dating book in that it's intended for both men and women—this stuff is fundamental and universal. We have a gender-oriented language, and I'm going to be talking about a lot of things in which gender is quite relevant as subtext, even when a statement can apply to someone of any gender or sexual orientation. When I refer to your partner, I don't know what gender your partner is, or what sexual orientation you have. "He/she" is awkward, "he" by itself seems like a sexist relic of our linguistic tradition, and "she" alone sounds a bit contrived as a reaction to the old tradition. So I will resort to the increasingly popular usage of "them" and "they" as versatile, gender-independent pronouns. If you're a language purist, this might bother you. I encourage you to get over that. Read this book, find a partner, have a better life, thank me, and let it go...

A QUICK NOTE ON PROPER NOUNS:

Some of the stuff in here is pretty personal, so while a few of the names I use are real, I've changed most names to protect people's privacy.

The stories in here are all real, and I've told them accurately as I understand them. All of the substance of the stories is there, but occasionally I've tweaked a detail to help obscure the identities of the people involved.

CHAPTER 1
FIND YOUR MOTIVATION

If you're like me, a partner is a priority. Sure, OK, you kick ass and you're independent and you've got your life set up. Cool...but still you want someone riding shotgun with you. Be clear on that point, and you'll find your motivation.

We're a social species. Relationships are very important to us. Back in 1939, a Harvard academic named George Vaillant helped start up the famous Grant Study, an examination of healthy aging by charting various factors over the course of the lifetimes of many subjects, all of them white, male, and American (it *was* 1939, after all...). More than half of the group were underprivileged young men from the Boston area, and the rest of the group were healthy Harvard undergraduates. Vaillant, his group, and their successors tracked the lives of all of these men from youth to old age, over the course of 75 years.

One thing that has come out of the study is that the most important predictor of long-term happiness among these guys, regardless of socio-economic standing, was the quality of their relationships. Who they loved and how they loved them. Vaillant has written a book about the study called *Triumphs of Experience*, and in it he summarizes: "Happiness is love. Full stop."

The study was about men, but this generalizes across the spectra of gender and sexual orientation. We all, to varying degrees, need love, acceptance, physical presence, camaraderie—all that good stuff. Sometimes we just need to know someone's there to help.

You probably have many kinds of relationships, any of which can be very important to you, including your family, your friends, your romances, your co-workers, and so on. All of them matter, but rarely are any of them as deep and intimate as a good romantic relationship. Having a deeply committed lover, whether or not you get married, is often the most direct route to happiness.

It's nice to have someone who is there just as a physical presence, to hold us, to touch us, to provide a sense of emotional security. Relationship therapist Dr. Aline Zoldbrod feels that touch—even non-sexual touch—is so important that she recommends her clients get regular massages if they don't have a loved one to hold them or caress them.

Of course sexual touch is good, too. We're hard-wired to want to reproduce, and our nervous system rewards us for engaging in sex, even in situations where actual reproduction won't or can't take place. It's not just a physical buzz, though. Sex can be a really good thing psychologically, too: it can be exciting, it can be validating, it can be warm, and it can be fulfilling. It's great to have a regular, healthy sex life, especially one based on love and affection, not only for the pleasure, but for the validation and reassurance of touch.

It's also nice to realize that somebody's got your back:

- When you do or say something stupid, your partner can stand up for you and comfort you. An embarrassing mistake at work or a humiliating social gaffe at a party can be rough on you. In times like those, it's really good to have someone who can help you put it in perspective and let you know that you're unconditionally loved.

- When you have an important decision to make, they can help you make it. They can offer a second opinion, they can spot a flaw in your assumptions, or they can enthusiastically agree with you and give you confidence that you're on the right track. Two heads are better than one.

- When a helping hand is needed for anything, there they are. Many hands make light work, but it's more than that. It's a comfort to know that you're part of a team, and that help is available, whether or not you actually need it.

- They're simply present. When Nancy is on the couch next to me and we're both working on our laptops, it doesn't matter whether or how often we talk—there's a fundamental comfort in her presence.

None of this is news to you. You just need to think about it, and be very clear with yourself about what you want out of life. If, like me, you feel certain that you'd be happiest with the right partner, then you should commit to finding that person. That doesn't mean you can't enjoy life without them—of course you can, and you should—but you should be honest with yourself, understand what it is you really want, and see if you can go get it.

My clients can tell you that I'm a big believer in articulation. We very frequently have stray thoughts about things we want or mean to do. These thoughts zip through our consciousness, sometimes repeatedly, but very frequently they get no more traction than that. Life intrudes, distractions abound, and time passes. I find it really helps to articulate these thoughts, whether that means writing them down, telling a friend or loved one, or simply saying them to the mirror.

Articulation helps focus the stray thoughts; it helps make them real, and helps us gain clarity. If we can articulate what we want, we have a better chance of getting it. If we can say what it is we mean to do, we have a better chance of doing it.

Do you want to find the right partner? Great—then tell yourself that, and don't be dissuaded from it. Write it down, or shout it to the rooftops. Whatever works for you.

Such articulation does not constitute a legally binding contract: you can and should continuously update your ideas, as you gain experience and insight, as you fine-tune what it is you want, as you come up with different approaches for getting it. But by all means, spell out what it is you're doing, and why you're doing it.

FIGURE OUT IF YOU'RE READY, AND THEN BE *READY*

Be honest with yourself. If you're ready for love, be ready for it.

If you've been fending off every potential partner with a broadsword, regardless of how terrific they might seem, it could be that you're just not ready for love, for whatever reason. Maybe you've seen close-up too many relationships that have gone awry, and you find it hard to trust either a relationship or yourself. Maybe you haven't yet gotten over your ex. Maybe you're consumed by your work, your family, your health, or something else going on in your life, and much as you like the idea of love in principle, it just isn't a high enough priority at the moment for you to be focused on it.

Whatever the reason, it's a reason, and you need to be very clear on whether you can give a relationship the emotional attention it deserves. Weigh your priorities, imagine your potential future, and do the right thing by yourself. Love matters, all right, but so does the rest of your life.

Be honest with yourself, however. Don't talk yourself out of it too easily: it might be that, even if you're scared, you'll review your assumptions and conclude that there really is no reason that you can't or shouldn't fall in love. Try to be ready sooner rather than later—don't stall if it doesn't serve you—but make sure you're ready.

Once you've weighed your priorities and know that you're there, give love a chance. A very interesting article appeared in the *New York Times* entitled "To Fall in Love with Anyone, Do This". Two people were discussing a study by Dr. Arthur Aron, in which subjects asked each other (and answered) increasingly personal questions. On top of that, the study subjects stared into each other's eyes for four minutes. The two people tried it, and sure enough, they fell in love. The headline of the article is a bit provocative and misleading, and the author notes that they might have fallen in love regardless, but by putting themselves in a vulnerable position with each other, they almost certainly facilitated the process.

That doesn't mean you have to do what they did, but the article highlights an important point: the more open you are to love, the more vulnerable to it you make yourself, the better your chance of experiencing it.

So all those rules you have about dating, or about not dating? Review them, and figure out what's at the root of them. Your handy little rules of thumb might not always serve you.

Kerri did not want to be set up. She'd been through it before; as a matter of fact, her best friend Gail had made a habit of setting her up. Problem was, these dates usually served Gail's interests more than Kerri's—it was an excuse to go somewhere, or it enabled a double date with someone, or something, but what it did not do was present Kerri with any guys she was really interested in. So Kerri had resolved not to put up with it anymore

Of course, Gail was no dummy, and she was catching on to Kerri's growing resistance. So when she figured out that Kerri and Ron would be great together, she got sneaky. She claimed that Ron, who like her was Jewish, didn't have any place to go for Passover Seder. (Omitting the little detail that Ron wasn't actually practicing and didn't give half a damn about Passover.) Moreover, Kerri's favorite poet was going to be speaking at this large community event.

So Gail gave Kerri her motivation, and made up a convincing motivation for Ron, and they drove with Gail's mother to the festivities.

Lacking seniority, both Kerri and Ron had to sit in the back seat of the car, where they got a chance to know each other during the two hour drive. Kerri was a history major, and, doing her own thing, was reading a shoemaker's journal from the 1850s. A what? Ron inquired about it, and didn't quite believe her. He thought it odd that she was reading such a thing, but at the same time it was interesting: it seemed that here was an independent, thoughtful woman.

On they went. More bonding took place over the meal. For years Gail had invited her best friend to their family seder , so Kerri was well acquainted with the ceremony. Ron, on the other hand, had only ever been to one Passover seder in his life. The upshot was that Kerri, the Irish Catholic girl from Yankee country in Ipswich, Massachusetts, was teaching the Jewish kid from the Bronx how to conduct himself during the seder.

After they'd gotten home, Gail pressed Kerri and Ron on what they thought of each other, and the answers were mostly positive but noncommittal.

So Gail kept at it, inviting the two of them to various things with no results, until one night when they were out at a club for a concert, Gail finally blurted to Ron, in front of Kerri: "This is your last chance! Just get her fucking phone number already!"

Thus put on the spot, Kerri and Ron sheepishly gave each other their phone numbers. And of course Gail wasn't going to let it stand there, so they used those phone numbers. Kerri and Ron began dating all by themselves, and they've been happily married for years.

Kerri says she never would have gone to that long-ago seder if she'd known it was a set-up. And that would have been a shame. Kerri's rules weren't serving her, but luckily she had a good friend to circumvent them for her. Please check your rules, understand why you have them and whether they apply in all cases, and keep yourself open to finding someone. Don't make Gail get involved.

GO OUT AND GET IT

Have you ever hoped that love would just happen for you? That'd be nice, of course, and it might happen, but it very probably will not ever happen unless you put in some effort. Here's the reason, and repeat after me:

"The world does not owe me a partner."

Try saying that out loud and saying it again. Remind yourself of it as often as you need to. The world doesn't owe you a partner, and it might never throw one in your way without a little effort on your part.

> *"Depend on the rabbit's foot if you will, but remember it didn't work for the rabbit."*
>
> –R.E. Shay

You have to actively find the right person. That might sound like work to you, but it's work that's well worth doing. This book is about putting in the right *kind* of effort.

Don't get me wrong—maybe the universe will come through for you. You *could* extend no effort whatsoever toward finding a partner, and you *might* get lucky anyway. Sweet. But you can't count on it. And you absolutely *shouldn't* count on it if you really do want to have a partner in your life. You've got to create your own luck. Keep your eyes on your goal, and go get it.

> *"Luck is the residue of design"*
>
> –John Milton

I started dating when the time came, and I took my lumps. I tried in vain to find someone who shared my passions, like shooting pool, birdwatching, or playing bridge.

There were lots of crusty old guys with bad habits in the pool halls. Not so many women there, though. And the few that I found there were either married or too young or not interesting to me or not interested *in* me. But the tables were good, and the beer was cold, and I had fun shooting pool.

There were more women who birded, but the trick was finding them. The bitterns and the rails that I was looking for were in some remote, lonely marsh, where as often as not nobody else was present. Maybe there would be a birder or two around, and maybe one of them would be female, but again with the married thing. Or they'd taken up birding after they'd retired and were decades older than me. I just wasn't meeting single birders. But the bitterns and the rails, to say nothing of the beautiful setting, were ample reward.

I've played cards all my life, and when I went to the place where they played duplicate bridge, I immediately saw that despite being in my 40s, I'd brought the average age down a good bit—fewer and fewer young people are playing it these days. And married couples make natural bridge partners, so lots of the players were already paired up and sniping at each other about decades-old disagreements on proper bidding. The one and only woman there who wasn't wearing a ring and caught my interest—smart, lots of personality, kinda cute—also turned out to have a partner already...a woman. The duplicate bridge game was clearly not going to be a pick-up spot. But the competition was good, and I had fun, and I got better at bridge.

So no women for me from my various pastimes. Does that mean that I was wrong to spend my time pursuing these things? Absolutely not! They made life livable at a low point in my life. They were the things that gave me joy. And just because I didn't find someone doing those things doesn't mean that I couldn't have found someone. I just needed some luck. There really are interesting single birders and bridge players and pool players out there; I just didn't happen to bump into them when I was single.

Regardless of the possibilities, I wasn't meeting women passively simply by doing the things I liked. I chatted with women at the supermarket, or in the line at the post office. A couple of times I even made bold to follow through and suggest an exchange of phone numbers or email addresses. I never got anywhere that way, but it didn't deter me.

What finally worked for me was online dating. What works for you might be something else entirely. The point is to make good things happen, when good things aren't just happening to you. The point is to give yourself your best opportunity.

SHORT-TERM GOALS ARE COOL...

It might be a while before you find that great partner, the one you could even imagine spending your life with. In the meantime, there's no reason you can't enjoy your relationships in the here and now.

Maybe you're lonely. You want someone to bring along to the company party. It might be nice to have *some* sort of sex life. And your soulmate is nowhere in sight. Don't worry about that—have whatever sort of relationship you want in the short term, as long as it doesn't interfere with your long-term happiness.

Nicole went from Massachusetts to college in New Orleans, and as a young, impressionable freshman, she met an Iraq war veteran who was ten years older than she was. This guy was from the bayou, a Cajun, and led a lifestyle that was entirely different from her own. He was hot: handsome and very physically fit (he was a body builder). And oh, yeah, he had a great personality. She had a terrific time with him.

The problem was, he came from a different background. One night they were out and he warned her: "If I grab you suddenly, it's so you don't get hurt." He went on to explain that, before he went to Iraq, he had been a drug dealer. (He got busted and, since he was already enlisted in the Marines, the judge gave him a choice between Iraq and jail.) Nicole shrugged it off, saying that she'd known a couple of kids who dealt pot, but he said "No, the real kind. Mercedes, scales, the whole bit." He knew he might be recognized, and if so, there might be trouble.

Another night they were at a bar, having a great time, and his friend came over to the table and said "I think there's gonna be some trouble." Which was probably a good call, inasmuch as he had broken a pool stick over the head of another guy, and that guy's friends were now there. They called in their own friends as reinforcements, and the bar owner, who'd heard all this, closed the bar down. Her boyfriend assured Nicole that it would be all right, because he had his gun.

They did succeed in getting out of there in one piece, but these were among many reminders that this was a very different world from the one she'd grown up in, and she felt she had to call off the relationship.

But here's the thing: Nicole was smiling throughout as she told me the story. She was very fond of him, and he was a ton of fun. It was a great adventure for her. So she didn't get a long-term relationship out of it, but years later she still refers to this time as "the best three months of my life."

You might have a story like that. OK, maybe not *quite* like that. But one in which you learned something, or gained a life-long friend, or just had fun, as Nicole did.

...BUT DON'T LET THE SHORT-TERM GET IN THE WAY OF THE LONG-TERM

Short-term goals should be just that. Your current relationship doesn't have to be your last one. Enjoy the present, while staying focused on the long term.

We can't focus enough on the word *focus*. Have all the fun you want, but don't let short-term relationships get in the way of longer-term relationships. Let your partner know if you want to keep your options open, and they might even be able to help you find your long-term partner. Not only do you skip a lot of drama and hurt feelings that way, but it gets you closer to your goal.

As important as it is that you're honest with others, it's even more important that you're honest with yourself about what you're doing. The important thing is to avoid settling into a relationship that you don't really care about, or one that you know can't work in the long term, if in doing so you're not leaving yourself open to finding the right partner.

IT'S NOT ALL ABOUT THE SEX (BUT SOME OF IT IS)

A word about sex: have it, or don't have it, but know what you're doing. And make sure your partner knows what you're doing.

This just in: sex is complicated, and it can mess with people's emotions in a big way. It can block you from finding the right relationship, it can leave you in pain, or it can leave you with regrets.

Having said all that, it sure can be fun. And at least one study suggests that having sex at least occasionally can help you make better decisions: if you've been sexually frustrated, you might find yourself falling into bed with someone who isn't right for you, and maybe getting too emotionally involved with them.

If you have sex with someone you're sure you won't get entangled with—a trusted friend, perhaps—you can solve this problem. The flip side of that is that if you have mind-blowing sex with someone you're not serious about, that can be a powerful drug, and can lead to questionable choices. The important thing is to be very aware of all that, and to know what you're doing going in. Trust your instincts: if something feels like a bad idea, or if you wouldn't want to discuss it with a friend, it probably really is a bad idea. If it doesn't feel that way, have a great time.

One of my clients had been sexually abused as a child, and not surprisingly, that made it hard for her sexual self to develop— when she'd had sex, it seemed like it was something that had to be managed, and was in service of whatever relationship she was in at the time. It wasn't a pleasurable end in itself.

There came a time when she hadn't had any sex in years. She'd always known in an intellectual way that not all men were like her abuser, and while she'd come to believe that the damage wasn't permanent, she felt that she needed to test that notion "in the field", as she put it.

So she decided she was going to have sex, and made the bold step of discreetly telling a few of her co-workers that she wanted some. One of her male co-workers emerged as a candidate. They liked each other, and while it was clear that they weren't ever going to have a serious relationship, they seemed compatible enough that a sexual liaison might be nice.

When the time came, it was surprisingly easy and pleasant. Though their tryst was strictly sexual, the shared vulnerability and intimacy felt almost sacred to her. They thoroughly enjoyed themselves, and agreed that their shared night was going to be the extent of the relationship. The whole experience was a huge relief to her, and freed her not to worry about sex as she approached her future relationships.

The moral of the story: have a great time. It's your body, and you get to use it as you see fit. Just do what feels like it's going to serve you in the long run. If short-term pleasure doesn't interfere with that, go for it.

BUDGET FOR SETBACKS, BUDGET FOR SUCCESS

If you budget for setbacks, you can budget for success as well.

Setbacks are gonna happen. The red-hot lover who suddenly vanishes on you. The one who inexplicably turns moody and cold, and won't say why. The surprising revelation that your partner thinks you're going to hell because you don't believe what they believe. All kinds of things can go wrong. Know that these sorts of things are coming, and when they happen, dust yourself off and continue. It's surprising sometimes how much easier it is to accept a setback if you've already acknowledged the possibility and put it in perspective.

Once you realize that setbacks are part of the equation, you don't have to place too much importance on them. They don't mean you won't succeed in the long run.

When I started dating at mid-life, I was ready for setbacks and disappointments. And boy, did I find them. I told you at the beginning of this book how many women I tried to make a connection with, and while I finally got the happy ending, please believe me when I tell you that it was pretty challenging along the way.

There were plenty of times when I felt like it was just me: I was unattractive, or too old, or clueless. Someone I thought should be perfect for me would show no interest. Someone whose online profile sounded ideal had no personality. Someone else would go out with me, be friendly and engaging and generally a lot of fun, and I'd get my hopes up. Then she'd vanish.

Other times I felt like it was just them: all the really good women were married, or lesbians, or both.

All the while I kept my eyes on the prize. I had a pretty good idea what happiness would look like, and I knew damn well what unhappiness looked like. So I kept going. And going.

One welcome outcome of the whole process was that I gained experience and perspective, so I learned to temper my expectations and anticipate that any given date wasn't particularly likely to lead anywhere.

It wasn't all bad. I had a handful of relationships of different sorts, and though none of them were really serious, I got good things out of them.

I had good sex for the first time in a very, very long time.

I made some really good friends, who are an important part of my life to this day. Some of them helped me through the rough patches, some of them taught me things, and some of them continue to share good times with us.

And of course I got the ultimate prize in the form of my wife, Nancy. I could spend several pages crowing about how terrific she is for me, but that's not the point. The point is that you can find somebody who is terrific for you. A genuinely happy ending, even the potential for a happy ending, trumps all of the pain and disappointment along the way.

Luck is capricious. Sometimes it seems like everything is going your way, or nothing is going your way. But it can certainly happen that your good luck will follow your bad.

Take Mike, for example. He'd just been through a long stretch in which he'd had two or three brief relationships that were unsatisfying and ultimately led nowhere. He was tired and feeling discouraged, and trying yet again to find someone new was the furthest thing from his mind.

When it came time to go on a Colorado River water-skiing weekend with a bunch of friends, that sounded just about right to him. He'd been doing it for years, and it was one of his favorite activities.

Meanwhile, one of his friends brought along another friend, named Nikki. Mike noticed right away that not only was Nikki cute, but she was smart, friendly, and had a sharp-tongued sense of humor that he enjoyed.

The group got their getaway started by going to a casino in Nevada to gamble, drink, and generally have fun. They had a good time, but had to pay the piper the next day, when they got up early to go waterskiing.

One of Mike's friends asked him to help out by going on a boat with a group of women who wanted to be together but didn't have much boat experience between them. The idea was that, since Mike had loads of experience driving boats, it would be good to have him on hand in case they ran into trouble.

Now, many of you are probably thinking that a single guy would be more than pleased to find himself on a boat with a bunch of young, attractive women. But as I said, Mike wasn't actively looking for a girlfriend. Moreover, he was still feeling the effects of the previous night, and he didn't know any of these women, and he wasn't going to be with his buddies. It all sounded more like responsibility and less like fun. But he agreed anyway, because it seemed like the right thing to do.

They got out on the water with one of the young women driving, and after a while her lack of experience showed. They were in the middle of the lake when she inadvertently backed the boat up over the tow line. The line got tangled in the in-board propeller, which was situated not behind the boat but underneath it. Mike knew what had to be done. He dove into the water, swam under the boat, and untangled the line from the propeller, all in one breath. He surfaced and got back on the boat, and they were up and running again.

The young women—including the aforementioned Nikki—were much impressed, and credited Mike with saving them. Even though he himself didn't see the situation as all that dire, he was clearly the hero of the day.

The ski trip carried on. At one point, as he was working on the boat, Mike's glasses fell off and into deep water, where there was no hope of recovery. This was a problem, because he needed his glasses to drive home to California. His friend Darren came up with a solution. He realized that Nikki lived in the same area as Mike, and so he recruited her to drive Mike's car and get them both home that way. Mike was a good friend of good friends, and since she'd gotten to know him a little on the boat, and since of course they all had a pretty favorable opinion of him by this time, she agreed to drive this guy home.

Well, you can guess the rest of the story. A long car ride gave them plenty of time to get to know each other, and plenty of time to flirt with each other. Things blossomed between them, and now they're married with kids. Nikki now accuses him of losing his glasses on purpose. She doesn't really believe that, but I suspect she wouldn't mind even if she did.

So when the setbacks happen—and they will, unless you're extraordinarily lucky—be ready for your luck to turn. Be open to meeting people. Give yourself every chance to make a romantic connection, and don't disqualify yourself because you think there's no way this gorgeous, fascinating person could possibly be interested in you. Remind yourself that consistently making connections can work. Somebody is out there that you can have a successful relationship with. It might take time, and of course there are no guarantees that you'll be in the right place at the right time to find one of your potential partners, but rest assured they're out there. Make success part of the plan, and keep working toward it, even when the going is slow.

BUDGET YOUR TIME

Prepare yourself for all of this to take a while. Not only might it take a long time to happen, but you might have to spend a lot of time along the way giving yourself the chance. You are wise to budget time for finding the right person, and even wiser to budget time for the right relationship to come to fruition.

Many of us have extremely full schedules, and the accelerating pace of life isn't helping. It is so easy to say that you don't have time to go out. Which is true, if you aren't making your love life a priority. And that might seem right to you. You might feel like you have to prioritize work (maybe), family (maybe), friends (maybe), and whatever else that seems serious and not so frivolous as dating.

But check your assumptions. Love is fundamental to happiness. Do all of those things really take precedence, all the time? Some will be more important than others, and maybe a few of the less important ones can be postponed, or skipped, or handed to somebody else to do.

And are you fully using all of those hours? Couldn't part of your time be spent doing an activity you enjoy doing, which just happens to give you a shot at meeting someone interesting?

Just as with money, investments of time can pay off. My former dental hygienist, Lucia, tells the story of meeting her husband. She was living in Gainesville, Florida at the time, and had a conference to go to in Miami. There she met Javier, who was helping to run the conference. They hit it off immediately, and a mutual attraction took hold. Over the course of that weekend they kept running into each other, and each evening they socialized with the group outside of the conference itself. All of that gave them the opportunity to get to know each other a little bit, and as things were wrapping up, they exchanged phone numbers.

They talked regularly over the next few weeks and started to develop real feelings for each other, but weren't able to get together right away because of the distance between their homes.

Finally they had an opportunity. Javier planned to drive the five hours from Miami to Gainesville for their first real date.

So far, so good. But in the meantime, a few of Javier's buddies had made plans to visit, unbeknownst to him. We might quibble with their lack of foresight in not discussing it with him, but that's a different story. There he was, faced with a dilemma. He didn't want to ruin the weekend for his buddies, nor did he want to miss out on keeping his date with Lucia, who he suspected was something pretty special.

He called and explained the situation to her. He was clear about wanting to see her, so he offered a solution: he would drive up to Gainesville, drive her back to Miami, put her up in a room of her own, and the two of them would spend a fun weekend with his friends.

Lucia too felt like Javier was a keeper, and she felt she knew him well enough to be comfortable accepting his offer, so she did. They both had a great time that weekend. Partly because of the fun things they did, but mostly because they really clicked together. It's amazing how much fun you can have when you're in the right company.

Of course, he still had to get her home when it was over, which was another ten-hour round trip. His friends thought he was crazy to drive such a long way, but Javier was no fool. The relationship took, and it wasn't long before Lucia was able to see her way clear to moving to Miami, where love blossomed and they ended up getting married.

In hindsight, that 20 hours of driving that seemed like so much to his buddies paid off in a big way. A terrific wife and four-year-old twins seems like a fantastic dividend.

So Javier used his time wisely. For Andrea and Jesse, it wasn't about time out of their schedule. It was about years out of their lives.

It took Andrea years to be really ready to find her partner. She'd had a string of relationships, and her friends couldn't see the commonality. She had been in her current relationship for three years when she knew she just wasn't heading in the right direction. So she signed up for a self-discovery program.

The experience was eye-opening. Andrea found the commonality: she'd gone for guys that she could help in some way, but it was deeper than that. Out of insecurity, she found herself drawn to guys that she felt somehow superior to. She realized that, though she hadn't given it the name before, her boyfriend was an alcoholic. What was more, she came to the startling and unsettling realization that she hadn't really wanted him to get better. She realized that not only was she enabling him, but that she was arguably toxic for him.

Thus wised up, she broke off that relationship, and started trying to work through her insecurities and date men who were her equal, or maybe even "better" than her somehow.

Enter Jesse. She had met him once before, and then one day at a party in Portland, they literally bumped into each other and turned to face each other. After they'd made their apologies, he said "Andrea, I'm Jesse, remember me?" Suddenly the noise and distraction of the party fell away for her, and they started an intense conversation.

They were both smitten, but were trying to play it cool, and respect each other's time. So each time they talked, they left off a great conversation, and resumed mingling. But the magnetic attraction was too strong, and they kept coming back together for more intense conversation, the kind where on more than one occasion she said to herself "I can't believe I just told him that."

Before long it became clear that they didn't need to fake it, and that they wanted to spend their time with each other. They decided to leave the party and skip the small talk with anyone else. They'd both arrived on bikes, so they rode through the backstreets of Portland, cruising the roundabouts with rose gardens in the middle.

It was, to wear out a cliché, a magical night. The next morning Andrea called her mother and said "Mom, I've met him."

This was that guy that she'd decided not to be afraid of. He was whip-smart, well-educated, worldly, good-looking, a talented musician, and socially adept. In short, the kind of guy she'd have been intimidated by a few years earlier. Now she was ready.

One out of two ain't bad: she was ready, but he wasn't there yet. He'd had the notion that he would never get married, never have children, never commit. Yet here was Andrea, and he was falling in love. Andrea was an educator, and had a year-long teaching obligation in Kenya and Belize coming up. Since Jesse wasn't the commitment type, they mutually decided that at this point it made sense for them to go their separate ways, and they officially broke off the romance.

The heart wants what it wants, however. They kept their distance, both literally and figuratively, if not emotionally. They communicated just once while Andrea was away. Jesse confessed that nothing had changed for him. By which he meant that he still loved Andrea.

Her interpretation was radically different: she thought he meant that the status quo still applied, that he didn't want to commit, and that they should stay broken up.

That might have led to a lifetime of regrets on both sides, but there was still enough gravitational pull that when she returned from Belize, they got together for a visit.

They started talking, and realized their miscommunication. Yikes! But no matter: here they were together again, and romance resumed. At this point Andrea made it very clear that she wanted this relationship, and she wanted Jesse to want it, too, and commit to her long term.

Nothing was resolved for a long time, but in the intervening months Jesse did a fair amount of soul searching. Along the way, two significant events occurred. His grandfather died, and Andrea came close to dying: she had an attack of acute appendicitis, and almost didn't make it.

That got Jesse's attention, and it made him think about the impermanence of life and what he wanted to get out of it. He knew that Andrea was part of what he wanted. He had long conversations with his own father and with Andrea's father, and he came to a decision.

It took him a full year, and Andrea was going crazy. Finally he found his resolve, and he started planning his proposal. They had another talk about commitment, and he said: "Do you need me to propose now, or can you wait for me to do it right?" Which of course was an indirect form of proposal and was all she needed to hear.

It was their usual practice to have tea together in the morning, and one day Jesse brought Andrea tea with something extra included. Andrea was groggy and didn't have her glasses on, and upon finding an engagement ring (which she didn't recognize) attached to the teabag, she said "What the heck?"

Every year they celebrate their "whatthecheckaversary."

It was a long and circuitous road for both of them, but the constant was that they were right for each other and loved each other. In the end, no amount of time was too much.

These anecdotes aren't to say that every investment of time is created equal. But love is worth the investment. Sometimes you have to take risks to earn rewards.

BUDGET YOUR MONEY

Just as you prepare yourself for spending time, prepare yourself for spending a few bucks.

When you decide to go for it, be serious about it. It might cost you some money, but spend it—within the constraints of your means.

If you've got a few extra bucks, go ahead and buy those new clothes you wanted anyway, or buy tickets to that great event you'd been longing to go to. Whatever it might be. If you don't have a few extra bucks, at least keep the principle in mind, so that when the time comes, you can make the right call about what to do with what money you have.

Just don't use money as an excuse to miss out on making connections. You're investing in yourself. One of my girlfriends-turned-friends took me out shopping to buy a jacket, and that jacket immediately impressed Nancy on our first meeting.

I was broke after my first marriage, and in the aftermath I began to really work on saving money. The good news for me was that the vast majority of my dates cost very little—sometimes it would be a free concert, often it would be a cup of coffee, and almost always it was something low-key and inexpensive.

So one evening a woman who I'd met on Match.com asked if we could meet for dinner at an expensive restaurant she liked. I offered to pay (as I usually did because it's a litmus test for some women), and she was glad to take me up on it. We got the appetizers, we got our entrees, we ordered drinks, and we got dessert.

I ended up spending a good bit more than I would have liked, especially since I had the feeling that this date wasn't going to lead to a relationship. I was trying to *save* money, not blow it on dead-end dates. I actually had the thought "I can't afford this."

I was mistaken.

Sure, if each and every date was as expensive as that one, it would have been much harder for me to save money. There was no way that was going to happen, though. It was still true that most of my future dates wouldn't cost too much. I actually did the math (told you I'm a numbers geek), and when I estimated how much I spent per outing, and figured out how many outings I would have if it took me another five years to find the right woman, it suddenly seemed manageable.

My estimate came to a few grand, which seemed like a bargain, if it meant I could find the love of my life. So I resolved to stop sweating it and just try to have a good time each time. Within two weeks, I met Nancy, and it all became a moot point.

CHAPTER 2
FIND YOUR FOCUS

"The perfect is the enemy of the good."

- Paraphrase of Voltaire quoting an unnamed Italian writer

Voltaire and that old Italian had it right in the quotation above. Sometimes we have an idealized vision of life that bears little resemblance to reality, but we invest so much in the vision that we refuse to accept less than perfection. In the process, we miss out on living the terrific *real* life that we could have had. It's not that we shouldn't have a vision at all; it's that we'll be happiest if we take a more flexible approach, and develop a more flexible vision, based on what we *really* want. So it's important to find our focus.

As I mentioned earlier, if you're going to find the partner you want, it's important to understand what you're looking for. I say *what* rather than *who* for a reason. People love the notion of having a soulmate, but when they talk about it, they act as if there's only one. If you think there's only one person for you out of the seven billion on the planet, your odds of bumping into them, much less getting to know them, are pretty low. The good news is that the truth is slightly different: there are many people somewhere out there who would make a great match for you. You don't have just one potential soulmate. There are *many* of them out there *somewhere*, and you have to get out there and put yourself in position to find one of them.

But you might not find them at all if you don't know what you're *really* looking for.

THE CHECKLIST

All right, let's talk about your checklist. You know the one I mean: that lengthy list of attributes that you want or even demand from any prospective partner.

1. Tall
2. Slim
3. Good-looking
4. Loves dogs
5. Makes good money
6. Dresses well
7. Between X and Y years old
8. Etc.

There are several problems with this sort of list. One is that, with each item, you're essentially making a generalization that disqualifies lots of very qualified partners. One of whom might have been terrific. Who might have given you a lifetime of happiness.

You're looking for a guy, and he must be tall? You're saying that you're not attracted to short guys, but think that through. I'm willing to bet that there's some short guy out there who you'd be wildly attracted to once you got to know him and figured out how cool he is.

You're looking for a woman, and she must be shorter than you? Same argument.

One of my clients is quite short, a little under five feet tall. Yet she thought she wanted a guy who was at least 5'10". I talked her through this a bit. It developed that she had a co-worker who was much shorter than 5'10", but she found him incredibly hot. He's married, but if he were single, she'd go out with him like a shot. So apparently *his* height wasn't important. Once I'd gotten her to think it through, she scratched that rule.

Let's also consider the case of Alexis. When she was in graduate school at the University of Washington, most of her colleagues were from somewhere far away. Given their proximity to each other and the demands of their work, they became a default social group. The gang would all convene at happy hour after their Wednesday graduate seminar.

Alexis became friends with all of them, but felt especially drawn to Kieran. The two of them hit it off right away, and soon she felt close to him. Just one problem: Alexis is 5'9", and Kieran is 5'4". She simply couldn't imagine them being together as a couple. She thought the option just wasn't available to her.

She knew he was a great guy, though, and even went as far as suggesting to her (shorter) roommate Wanda that maybe she should go out with Kieran. Wanda wasn't blind, though, and said "Maybe you should." Alexis reiterated her mantra: "That wouldn't work. He's shorter than me."

Fortunately, Kieran didn't feel limited by his height. He knew that he and Alexis were great together. He kept that option open, and let Alexis know that he wanted more than just friendship. She kept putting him off, until one weekend when the gang went camping up at the Paradise campground on Mount Rainier.

Maybe it was the activity, maybe it was the thinner air, maybe it was a little bit of alcohol that they'd brought along. Whatever it was, Alexis suddenly felt the possibility too. As they sat together alongside a stream, she felt closer to him than ever. So she got closer still, and kissed him, and kissed him some more. It just so happened that they had a tent handy....

Down came the barriers, and they officially started seeing each other. One barrier still stood, however: her parents objected, simply on the basis that they looked wrong together, and they imagined it would be hard for their little girl to overcome societal expectations about height. Their reaction was what was actually hard for Alexis, who considers herself something of a people-pleaser and had always tried to make her parents happy. But by this time she'd spent a lot of time with Kieran, and understood the unimportance of their relative height: "It didn't matter in bed and it didn't matter in life."

Her parents eventually saw how happy she was and got over their initial reservations. Alexis notes that height discrimination, especially vis-à-vis straight couples, is one of the few remaining prejudices that are socially sanctioned: people carry without question the expectation that the man will be taller than the woman. Others might look at them with surprise, and might think they're "wrong" for each other, but it doesn't feel like an issue to them at all.

Mark Twain once said "All generalizations are false, including this one." He meant that they're flawed and therefore dangerous, but they're occasionally useful nevertheless. Most of the items on your checklist encapsulate some truth, or at least an individual experience, but they typically narrow your view in ways that aren't helpful, and they can lead you to rule out good potential partners for bad reasons. Which can lead you to being pretty lonely.

Our friend Elise told me a story of a friend of hers who in her 20s had a list of ten "Cees": considerate, cash, Catholic—she didn't remember the rest. Maybe cute, courageous, whatever. If you think about it, you can see that every one of those criteria narrows down the list of candidates. By the time you're through 10 (or more) requirements, you'll be left with very few potential soul-mates. If you don't cross paths with any of those very few, or if they turn out not to be right for you despite meeting all your criteria, then what? You're out of luck. Over stupid stuff.

Let's take a couple of those Cees. Cash? How about someone who doesn't have much but also doesn't spend much and is smart, funny, kind, and completely adores you? And makes your life better in all kinds of ways apart from buying you stuff. Is that all bad?

Catholic? Was that really entirely necessary for her? Maybe, I guess, but I'm thinking the vast majority of people could make it work with somebody outside their denomination. What did this item on her checklist really mean? Was it about raising their kids in her denomination? Was it about a moral tradition? Or was it simply a desire to have someone with a similar background? Think through whether you couldn't be happy with someone who has slightly different beliefs from yours.

The point is, rigidity doesn't serve you. If you insist on a list and an incredible person comes along who doesn't quite meet one of your criteria, you might pass them by. Do you really want to pass them over and instead pick someone who is fractionally hotter or has a better resume but is otherwise not a good fit for you?

Our friend Anna set up two of her friends, Lara and Ben. They were two legal nerds with similar backgrounds who seemed perfectly matched in lots of conventional checklist ways. So Anna was shocked when Lara told her that she wouldn't accept a second date with Ben because he drove too fast. She said: "I'm not going to marry someone who will probably be killed in a flaming wreck."

Instead Lara ended up marrying someone who observed the speed limit more conscientiously. But there's far more to a relationship than sound driving habits. She later discovered that he really wasn't a nice person at all, and in particular he wasn't nice to her. Lara ended up divorcing him. By then Ben was long gone. She might have missed out on a great opportunity for a lousy reason.

So it's not just about passing up the right one because of your checklist; there's also the danger that the checklist will lead you to the wrong one. You can follow your list faithfully, and you might be unable to resist the temptation of someone who checks all the right boxes, whether or not they're the right person for you. Jane found Keith, an actor with everything she wanted in a guy: he was physically attractive, outgoing, funny, flamboyant, and had tons of personality. She was more than happy to sign up for all of that, and she moved in with him.

She didn't read the fine print, though. He was self-absorbed. He perhaps took his dramas too seriously because he wanted life to be like a Hollywood movie, and he was bitterly disappointed whenever it fell short. His disappointment affected his world view, and it affected their relationship. Jane wanted out. He wasn't the right man for her, regardless of how well he matched her checklist.

People are sometimes naïve about their expectations for their partners. You might not be immune. So take a little time and think about what's on your list and which of those things could maybe come off.

A FEW CRITERIA THAT REAL PEOPLE HAVE USED TO DISQUALIFY POTENTIAL PARTNERS:

- *"Guys with beards have something to hide."*

- *"I won't date anyone who wears blood-red nail polish."*

- *"Did you see his shoes??"*

- And my all-time favorite: *"If I open the car door for her, and she doesn't reach over to open the other door for me, I cross her off the list."*

- Fill in your favorites: there are a million more.

OK, here's an exercise for you: make up a checklist of all the attributes your dream lover would have. Put a star next to each of the attributes that's non-negotiable. As you continue through this book, revisit your list and consider whether you really need those attributes that don't have stars next to them. The ones that are needlessly restricting your choices. And keep an eye on the starred items, too, and see whether you can do without any of them. Your results may vary, but there's a pretty good chance that you'll be able to live without some of them.

THOUGHT EXPERIMENT: Consider some of those nice-to-haves
that either are still on your list or once seemed important to you.
Then think about a person you find personally attractive, the kind you
could almost see yourself with if only they were available. Ask yourself
whether they're missing any of your nice-to-haves. Repeat this exercise until you find a quality and a person it applies to. Then maybe you
can remove that item from your list.

THE REVISED LIST

"So what should I really be looking for?" you ask.

Let's start a new list:

1. Character

2. Rapport

...aaaaaand we're done.

These are really the only two things you need from a partner.
Let me explain.

CHARACTER

What do we mean by character? Lots of things, actually. But
mostly they are intrinsic qualities that make a person admirable
and worthy of respect, to you or to anyone else. Look for things
such as kindness, consideration, and responsibility. In this section
we're talking about looking for these things in others, but let's be
fair—we should look for them in ourselves as well, and be conscious of giving as good as we get.

KINDNESS

First and foremost, your partner should be kind. It would be nice if they were kind to everyone, but it's crucial that they are kind to you. Consistently kind to you. I mean that. If they're not, you should find somebody else. Even if you're not sure you can find somebody else, you're better off being single. Please don't subject yourself to anyone who isn't kind to you, no matter how admirable they seem to others, no matter what sort of tortured genius they might be. If your partner isn't kind to you, you almost certainly won't be happy.

Sometimes people you're just meeting don't fully reveal themselves. They might be on their best behavior in the courting phase. But if at any point you notice that they're being unkind, stop and consider what's going on.

Unkind things that *nobody* should be doing to you, much less your prospective partner:

- *Mean-spirited insults.* If your partner teases you in a gentle and joking way, fine—use your judgment. If the teasing is hurtful, ask your partner to dial it back. And if they don't, you might want to dial back your relationship with them.

- *Violence.* Absolutely no violence. Not even a tiny bit.

- *Yelling and snapping.* This one can be hard for people who are accustomed to interacting in this way. Maybe you can chalk it up to a bad habit, but it's unkind and unnecessary. Encourage your partner to communicate positively, and with patience. After a while it can become habit.

- *Deliberately pushing buttons.* If your partner does or says something that serves no real function except to piss you off, ask them to cut it out.

- *Ignoring things that are important to you.* Also tricky. It's one thing to be uninterested, but it's another to make no effort at all. Even if your partner doesn't share your passions, they can be supportive of them.

Emily Esfahani Smith wrote a good article for *The Atlantic Monthly* in 2014 that encapsulated research about the importance of kindness in communication between partners. It was a fairly stark illustration of the difference in divorce rates between couples who were kind and accepting of their partners, and those who were cold and contemptuous. Her conclusion: unkindness kills relationships, and kindness makes them work.

CONSIDERATION

Your lover should be considerate. Note that consideration is a bit different from kindness. It means that they should be aware of you, aware of your feelings, aware of the basic niceties of life. Someone can have a heart of gold but be completely oblivious to others, and they might do and say things that are hurtful to you as a result. Not good. I'd say this isn't quite as important as kindness, but it's still important.

Ways that your partner should demonstrate consideration:

- *Being aware of your feelings.* If they know something hurts you or stresses you out, they should recognize it and either avoid doing it if they can, or at the very least help you work through your feelings.

- *Being aware of your physical needs.* If you have allergies, they should know what they are. If you have limitations such as trouble lifting things, they should pick up the slack for you. If you're sick, they should do what they can to make sure you're getting the medical attention you need.

- *Being aware of your physical needs, part 2.* If your sex life has been slow, and you're frustrated, ask them if they can see their way clear to perking things up a bit. If they're not interested in at least discussing it, that's a problem.

- *Being aware of external pressures and expectations.* If, for example, you were raised in a family that celebrates a certain holiday in a certain way, your partner should decide whether they can support that tradition. In arriving at that decision, they should err on the side of kindness and consideration.

RESPONSIBILITY

Your partner should be responsible. You should be able to rely on them to do what they say they'll do, to show up when they say they will, to do the right thing, and to hold up their end of the partnership. They should be able to justify their actions to you and to themselves.

Ways your partner can demonstrate responsibility:

- *Earning their keep.* This might involve making money, doing housework, lending emotional support, whatever. Just make sure that they're contributing something that makes life better for you.

- *Not doing things that put you in a compromising situation.* This doesn't have to be a felony or a misdemeanor;

it could be something like embarrassing you needlessly, or doing something that undercuts you at work. Anyone can make a mistake, but if they do this sort of thing often, and especially if they don't seem to care, that's a red flag.

- *Consistently showing up when they say they will.* There will always be exceptions, but the pattern should be clear.

- *Doing what they say they'll do*, or having a good reason for not doing it.

- *Explaining themselves.* Whatever it is they're doing, they should be able to justify it. Really justify it—no rationalizing, no excuse-making, no misleading. You should genuinely believe in their justifications, and if they feel funny too often, that might be a red flag.

RAPPORT

And what do I mean by rapport?

It's a combination of mutual attraction, mutual respect, comfort in each other's presence, and joy in each other's presence. It's all about their connection with you. Of course you won't really mind if your partner happens to be smoking hot. But if you're crazy about someone, you'll enjoy looking at them and will find their otherwise ordinary appearance to be rather appealing. And if your smoking hottie turns out to behave like a jerk, their looks won't seem so important. I'm sure you can think of someone you really don't like who you'd concede was good-looking. Appearance is only one small part of the whole.

If you don't enjoy the company of your partner, that's a serious problem.

If your partner speaks to you contemptuously, that's a huge problem. And it says something about their character.

Denise is a professor of English literature at a mid-sized state university, and she also writes historical fiction aimed at middle-grade children. She met Todd online, and they arranged a date. When they met, he was everything she could hope for: smart and well-employed (he was a doctor), sweet and charming. He asked her about herself and seemed genuinely interested in her answers.

On their second date, the conversation turned to the home schooling she did for her children. He seemed critical of it and worried aloud about socialization, as people who don't know about home schooling frequently do, especially when they don't trust a parent to have thought about that. It was annoying, but she figured she could excuse his ignorance of the topic, and they otherwise had a nice time.

On date #3, he raised the issue of home schooling again, and since she's an English professor, he figured that she wouldn't be able to teach her children math or science. (Fill in your response to that here...) Again, she could pass it off as simple ignorance on his part, but afterward she realized that she was irritated after both of the last two dates.

On their fourth date, they met for dinner, and he announced that he'd been up until 2 o'clock the previous night, and she didn't have any interpretation of that. He pressed. "Aren't you going to ask why?" He couldn't wait to inform her that he'd spent hours researching hairstyles for her. He thought he'd helpfully remake her for the new year.

Denise wasn't impressed. He asked if she cut her hair herself, and when she curtly replied that she had a hair stylist, Todd asked if she liked her stylist. By now she was pretty well fuming, and dawn was beginning to break in Todd's consciousness. At least he was apologetic, but that didn't stop her from being angry all week.

They'd already scheduled a next date before he brought up the hair, and she gave him one last chance, although in hindsight she's not sure exactly why.

This time, he asked about her writing. Good, right? Well, that all depends on the question. He wondered if she'd be interested in writing a "real, hard-core novel."

He went on to mansplain to Denise, a professor of English literature, how there were two kinds of novels in the world, historical fiction and mainstream fiction. She was floored, and didn't know quite how to respond. He figured that historical fiction was relatively easy because you were just riffing off of actual events, but that mainstream fiction was pure imagination. In his weighty opinion, that was an important distinction. Thoughtful of him to offer her a way to improve herself, huh?

Todd pretty well hung himself with the too-ample rope that she allowed him. She left that date angrier than ever, but that didn't deter Todd from emailing her pictures of hairstyles she might consider.

Denise began to suspect that she was on Candid Camera. There was no sixth date.

Obviously Todd didn't show Denise the basic peer-to-peer respect that she needed to feel from him. If you don't feel genuine respect from someone that you're involved with (or, just as important, if you don't feel respect *toward* someone), the relationship is very unlikely to work.

Nora has a different sort of relationship. She had a list that included the following. What immediately jumps out at me is that most of the items on her list arguably fall into one or both categories of character and rapport. We can assume by their inclusion that most of these items are qualities she sees in herself.

- Spiritual, but not religious (rapport)

- Eats healthy food (rapport)

- Takes good care of himself (rapport)

- Sense of humor (rapport)

- Compassionate and caring (character)

- Likes to be physically active (rapport)

- Adores me (rapport)

- Intelligent (rapport)

- Loves himself and others (character)

- Likes being around women (character and rapport)

- Good listener (character and rapport)

- Self-aware (character)

OK, this list might be just a trifle specific, and we might quibble with one or two items, but it has the virtue of being mostly composed of things that really do matter, not arbitrary and inconsequential preferences.

And each of them just happens to apply to her husband, Dirk. Well done, Nora!

...AND MORE RAPPORT

The rapport was obvious between Matthew and Laura, who are in some ways the poster children for this book.

Matthew walked into a bar, and Laura immediately noticed him and thought he was attractive. He noticed her as well, and soon they were smiling at each other. Smiles are usually welcome, but some smiles are better than others. With the green light Laura was getting from Matthew, she departed from her usual practice and walked over to meet him.

While Matthew was impressed by Laura's pretty smile, he was even more impressed at how much fun she was to talk to. They spent a wonderful few hours together, and when it was time to go their separate ways, they exchanged contact information and agreed to be in touch. When the evening was over, Matthew found himself feeling eager and excited at the prospect of talking to her again.

He didn't see any point in playing games. He called her the next day. They immediately started dating, and Matthew has gotten to talk to her every day since.

About six months in, it was time for Laura to go off to Japan, where she had committed to teach English. They say absence makes the heart grow fonder, and that seemed to work in this case. They talked often, they wrote letters, and they longed to be together again.

So sure of their relationship were they that, after she'd been gone for four or five months, Matthew actually moved in with Laura's brother, and they remained roommates for over a year.

It was all about rapport for them, despite the fact that they might defy other people's expectations for them. Matthew is black and Laura is white. She reports that people are often surprised when they meet her husband because they simply assume that he's white. Sometimes they see her daughter and are confused about who she belongs to.

That's those people's problem; it's just not an issue for Matthew and Laura. He grew up in DC and had a very heterogeneous set of friends. A homogeneous set of friends actually makes him uncomfortable: from his perspective, the more diversity, the better. So he had no fixed expectations for what his future partner should look like.

Similarly, Laura grew up in a diverse environment. Her brother -in-law is Indian, and her brother's girlfriend is Korean. As a result, she had no fixed expectations for her future partner, either. She knew what she liked, and when Matthew walked into that bar, she liked him.

Notice what's missing from this story? There is no consideration of Mr. Right or Ms. Right, at least not in terms of externalities. They just really liked each other. There was no big first date; they didn't need one. There was no attempt at seduction. That would have been superfluous, because they just clicked. There was zero game-playing. Laura liked Matthew's smile and Matthew liked Laura's smile, and that was enough of a spark.

Laura didn't play any flirt-and-tease games. She didn't act dis- interested. She didn't worry about how hard to get she was or wasn't. She didn't maneuver herself to give him an opportunity to approach. Laura bravely approached Matthew and gave herself a great chance to connect with him.

He liked her and he liked talking to her, so Matthew didn't worry about how many days he was supposed to wait to call her. He didn't feign ambivalence and make her wait around, hoping and wondering. He wanted to see her again, so he called her and let her know that.

Of course it isn't always this easy, and it might never be so easy for you. But it's a great model to keep in mind.

It wasn't so easy for Caroline and Rob, for example.

Caroline was cast as Anna in a high school production of The King and I, and Rob was cast as Prince Chulalongkorn. They saw each other every day for weeks in rehearsals, and that made it easy for them to know each other. One day, as she was getting ready to drive home, she found a message under her windshield wiper that said "You're a great lady." She was touched, and she kept the note in her wallet, but for a long time she didn't know who'd put it there. She had her suspicions, however, and eventually put the question to Rob. He was a little evasive, but it was clear that he was the culprit, and Caroline was impressed.

When the play ended, the obligatory cast party took place, and Rob, not wanting to miss his opportunity, asked Caroline if she wanted to do something sometime.

She did.

They were different types—Caroline was a shy, introverted, rule-follower, whereas Rob was a boisterous, cavalier jock type—but their rapport was obvious. She enjoyed his sense of humor, and they always had fun together.

It came time to go off to college, and they ended up in different places, separated by the entire width of North America. They maintained a relationship by swapping two journals and communicating with each other that way; it allowed them to be spontaneous with their thoughts. Additionally, they talked on the phone once or twice a week.

As rosy as this seems, Caroline understood a few things: they started their romance at a very young age, they were still learning and growing, and marriage could be difficult, as she'd seen through the challenges that her parents had faced. So she was concerned about commitment, and they agreed to keep things open and see other people. When they were wrapping up their studies, Caroline could see a sort of commitment deadline coming, and she still wasn't too sure about the whole marriage idea, so she broke up with Rob.

He wasn't sold on the idea: he felt like it was based on fear and not rapport. Still, he honored her decision, and they started to get on with their lives.

Caroline had gotten close to a friend from school, and tried a romance with him. He was a great guy, but what he wasn't, was Rob. Her feelings just weren't the same. She still felt psychologically committed, despite her cold feet.

She realized that what she'd been feeling was a general fear, not a Rob-based fear. Caroline realized that if she kept avoiding a commitment, she might risk the possibility that Rob wouldn't wait around, and that she might lose him forever. She wouldn't know what she'd missed out on until it was too late.

The good news was that in insisting on their independence, she'd shifted perspective. Now she could consider life with Rob without feeling like it was something she "had to" do. As accustomed as she was to following the rules, marriage was too important to just accept as an obligation. Instead she was able to consider what a great time they'd always had together, and she could actively choose to commit to him, as momentous as that decision seemed. That perspective made all of the difference.

She got back in touch with Rob. Would he be willing to give it another chance? He'd felt the rapport, too, and claimed that he always knew she'd be back, but he had to protect himself. He wanted to make sure that Caroline wasn't going to jerk him around anymore.

When it was clear that she was all in, he was all in, too. And the sense that they belonged together has been there ever since. There's still work to be done: they both have strong personalities, and Caroline says that neither of them back down, they just "reposition." What serves as the foundation of their long and happy marriage is the way that they so consistently have fun together and enjoy each other's company.

They say love conquers all, and of course that's not always true. But love based on a genuine rapport can overcome a great deal, as it did for these two.

THE NICE-TO-HAVES ARE NICE TO HAVE

Some part of you has probably been objecting all along. "B-b-b-ut...attraction matters, doesn't it? What if the items on my list are really important to *me*?" Having said all that I just said, you're right. Sorta.

Attraction absolutely *does* matter. Sexual attraction is an important binding agent; you can argue that it's *the* most important binding agent: after all, the concept of a couple in our culture is understood to imply that the two are sexual partners. We assume that they are currently having sex with each other, or will be having it soon, or maybe, if they're of a certain age, they had a lot of it in the past.

Keep in mind that attraction doesn't have to happen all at once, and it can mean different things: it's not merely physical. By all means make sure you're attracted to a potential partner; just don't make too many assumptions in advance about the sort of person you'll be attracted to.

There is absolutely nothing wrong with appreciating physical attraction, or with appreciating the presence of those other little arbitrary items, such as taste in shoes, height, or eye color. If they pull the two of you together, terrific. The more of those things are present, the easier it will be to see your way clear to giving someone a try.

FINDING AUTHENTIC CONNECTION

Now that you've revised your list and are focused on the right things, you have to follow through. You have to think in terms of connection first. That can be hard to do in our superficial culture.

Ryan was conscious of how difficult it could be to find an authentic connection. Ryan is gay, and the popular gay dating sites were rather limited and rather tawdry: they seemed to be more about dick pics and bank accounts than they were about personalities, character, and priorities. Shirtless photos were the norm, and many sites wouldn't even show face pictures, because of people being closeted.

Ryan wasn't wild about meeting guys that way, but he didn't just lament the situation and leave it at that. He's enterprising, and he actually *did* something about it.

He went to work creating an online community called scene404 that allowed gay men to get together and get to know each other. In its initial conception, it was more about social networking than it was about dating, and it focused on community and shared activities.

Ryan discovered that he wasn't alone in his desire to relate to people in an authentic way. There were plenty of guys who felt the same way he did about the traditional gay sites, and they gravitated to his new online community. Because it seemed like a healthier way to meet prospective partners, it gradually morphed into a de facto dating site.

One guy who happened across Ryan's site early on was a programmer named Alan, and he was interested in the nuts and bolts of how the site was put together. They talked a bit of shop online, about software architecture and technologies and such. Along the way, Ryan discovered that Alan shared some of his iconoclastic political ideas, and that he was an interesting guy all around.

It wasn't long before the two of them had a meaningful friendship based on more than shop talk. Their sharing of thoughts and ideas led them to conclude that they were on to something here. Their conversations led to deepened feelings, which ultimately led to a relationship.

Which ultimately led to their marriage.

As their relationship had been growing, the popularity of the site continued to grow, and it became kind of a big deal. Eventually the site was acquired by OKCupid, which seemed like a pretty big win from a business perspective.

But that return on investment wasn't the half of what Ryan got out of the whole thing: the authentic connection he hoped to create for others ultimately resulted in an authentic connection for himself, and he found Alan.

FEAR THE HEAT

Earlier we established that the nice-to-haves are nice to have. Of course, the flip side of that is that you might be smitten by the person who hits all of those little arbitrary points, but it turns out that they're lacking something in terms of character and rapport. And in your smitten state, you'll have a hard time spotting the ways in which they're not right for you.

Dee was fresh out of a marriage that didn't quite work, and was ready to try something new. An old friend of hers just happened to be around and available, and this old friend just happened to be smoking hot. Not only did he look good, but he was great in the sack. Lots of fun...for a few days.

Then his flaws started to emerge. He was broke. He had substance abuse problems. He was uncommunicative and unkind. But he had a good sob story that made her sympathetic and, well, there was still the sex.

Before long he had thoroughly insinuated himself into her life, and when one day he'd kinda/sorta moved himself in, she wasn't prepared to move him right back out. In fact, she didn't even realize he'd actually moved in until his previous roommate (an old Navy buddy) told her that he had. Oh, and along the way, her friend managed to alienate his previous roommate, who promptly got himself a new one.

So there's her smoking hot live-in lover, with no money, no credit, no prospects, and no other friends to turn to. At this point Dee felt stuck with him. And not only was she stuck with him, but he was irresponsible--he would do things like leaving doors wide open, which her ex would then have to close when he stopped by to look after the dog. (I know what you're thinking, and yeah, the ex didn't look so bad at this stage.) Ultimately, she was able to get rid of the guy, but it wasn't easy, and she was kicking herself the whole time.

Earlier we talked about the value of having fun, but you need to understand what you're getting into, so that the fun stays fun and doesn't turn into something not very fun at all.

Mia has had the ostensible good fortune to go out with a lot of attractive men. Looks mattered to her, as they matter at some level to most of us. Most recently she spent a couple years with a guy who was very good-looking and who had been successful and happy in the past. It seemed to have potential, but by the time they met, his career had gone south and he'd lost confidence and motivation. That took its toll on the two of them: he struggled with even being in a relationship. She now realizes that it was never good, and that she probably stayed with him too long because he was so attractive.

Enter Nick, who Mia met online. Because he was in a public position, he didn't upload a profile picture. They corresponded for a while, and something was getting started. Before they met, he stipulated that they should have a two-date minimum to take the pressure off the first date. (Sound familiar?) That was a good move, because when they did meet, she was unimpressed by his appearance—average looks, a few extra pounds, not the kind of guy she was used to going for.

But because Nick asked for the time for Mia to get to know him a little, and because she honored that, she had the time to begin appreciating how terrific he is. He's smart, kind, interesting , and travels around the world doing charitable work. He opened up her world. If she'd just glanced at a picture in a profile and had applied her usual standards for appearance, she might still be in an unhappy relationship, instead of a happy one with Nick.

So beware the heat. It's a lot of fun, and if it's with the right person, it can be wonderful. The point is not to choose a partner based on the wrong reasons, and not to rule anyone out for the wrong reasons, either.

BEWARE THE COMFORT ZONE

The comfort zone, almost by definition, seems like a desirable place to be. And it is. We like comfort. Comfort is good.

For that very reason, it can be seductive. And therein lies the trouble. It's all too easy to get into a relationship because it seems comfortable, and not because it's the right connection. Romance is scary. Committing to a long-term relationship with another human being can be terrifying. How much easier it all seems if you feel like what you're getting into is something familiar, something manageable.

Take Heidi, for example. She'd been working in LA, but felt out of place there. She started considering other possibilities. When the right opportunity arose, she transferred to the suburbs of New York, which was more like her original home of Philadelphia, and also put her closer to friends and family.

When she first moved, she didn't know anybody in her new location in Westchester County. She had always been close to her sister, who lived in Boston, and so she ended up visiting her frequently. During these visits, she got to know her sister's circle of friends, and became part of the group.

Over time she and one of the guys gravitated to each other. They ended up sitting together almost constantly, and they tended to stay up later than the others. They often had time alone, and the gravitational pull increased. One of those late nights, they kissed.

Heidi was in her late 20s at this point, and she had an agenda. She wanted kids, she wanted a house, she wanted the sort of life you were supposed to want. Now here was Colin. He was nice, he was fun, and he was kinda cute.

He worked in a related field, so they had that in common. She even liked his family, who seemed supportive and reliable, and since they liked to entertain, she got to know them reasonably well.

In short, Colin fit nicely into Heidi's expectations of a boyfriend, and he slipped very neatly into the comfort zone. He had come pre-approved by her sister (ALERT: this is not as reliable as you might think) before they even started, and he spoke and acted in ways that were familiar to Heidi. They started a long-distance relationship.

He seemed a lot like her dad in terms of socialization and the way he laughed, and shared her father's interest in wine and fine dining.

After they had been seeing each other for six months, it seemed to Heidi that they should come to some sort of decision about what they were doing. After all, she was in her late 20s, and she wanted to get on with the aforementioned agenda.

Here's where the comfort zone really came in to play. The comfort zone that Colin represented enabled her to justify moving in with him in Boston. The comfort zone made him seem like a perfectly reasonable choice. She was vaguely aware that she wasn't as excited about life with Colin as she was supposed to be, but she actually had the notion that if it wasn't to be this guy, then who? Maybe she'd feel the same way about any guy. And this one was comfortable.

Things were fine for a while. Not great, but fine. They started a family; they bought a house.

Exit the comfort zone. When she and Colin first got together, he seemed maybe 30% like her dad. As the demands of life encroached upon them, he started to seem like maybe 80% like her dad. And that included alcoholism and anger issues.

He wasn't good at responsibility, which wasn't such a problem when they were just dating. It was a bigger thing when decisions about children had to be made, and when they needed paternal involvement, and when the mortgage had to be paid.

They muddled through, but the pressures mounted and the cracks in the relationship began to show. Their marriage deteriorated, and it ended in divorce.

Of course, marriages are often challenging, but Heidi feels like this one was predictable in some ways; she just didn't have the experience to predict it herself when she was in her 20s. Now she can clearly point to the comfort zone as the thing which facilitated the relationship and encouraged them to embark on a mediocre relationship, which ultimately turned into a deeply unsatisfying relationship.

Her experience doesn't mean that being comfortable with someone is a bad thing. It absolutely isn't—it's nice to have shared vocabulary and shared experiences, shared world views, shared tastes, common things to discuss and appreciate. It makes any relationship easier, and that's not a bad thing.

You just need to be aware that you're in it. And you need to understand what it means for you. If you're in a relationship simply because it's comfortable, and not because of a deeper connection, then the comfort zone might not always be your friend.

SETTLING AND THE UNDATEABLE

Many people are fond of the phrase "Why should I settle?" Let's parse that question.

First, we have to understand what we mean by settling. It might mean that somebody isn't wealthy enough, isn't good-looking enough, isn't whatever enough. If you can have somebody who is your dream in every regard, and the character and rapport are there, and they're completely into you, congrats. You've won the lottery. But you don't need all of those things to have a great partner and a great life together.

There is a book called "Undateable: 311 Things Guys Do that Guarantee They Won't Be Dating or Having Sex." This might be quite useful information for a guy who wants to improve his odds, but it's a pretty lousy list for someone to use when they're in search of a guy. Don't like his tighty whities? Buy him some boxers...or just get over it. Don't like his facial hair? If he's a terrific kisser, you could probably get used to it really fast. Someone might consider someone who does even a single one of these things to be undateable, and that's just silly. Almost all of the 311 things on the list have very little bearing on his character and even on your potential rapport. Of course the same applies to women, and to whatever it is you might not like about their clothes, their tastes, or their hobbies.

Abby got a job as a newspaper reporter. Office space was at a premium, and the only spot available to her was sitting with the news assistants.

One day Martin came over to chat with the assistant next to her. The observant Abby immediately spotted some flaws:

- He had a long ponytail. Tsk, tsk.

- He nattered on about a golf ball going through his windshield, which seemed to Abby like self-pity.

- In the course of that same conversation, he mentioned a relationship he'd had with a fashion model (how shallow!).

Three strikes, and Martin was undateable.

The news assistant, on the other hand, was a talented writer, very handsome, and *troubled*—basically catnip for Abby. They started seeing each other. Along the way, she got to know Martin through his regular visits to talk with her new boyfriend. They got to be friends themselves, and at one point Martin, who was the pitcher on the company softball team, recruited her to be his catcher. (Metaphor alert!) They got comfortable enough with each other that they planned collaborative projects that they might work on together, although the newspaper never quite cooperated. They were solidly in the friendship zone.

Fast forward a few years, and the news assistant was yesterday's news. Now Abby was working for a big software company and so was Martin. Friendship renewed.

One day they were chatting and comparing weekends. His involved a four-car fire, and he needed to swing by the junkyard after work to grab some stuff out of his ruined car. He invited her along, and she had the thought "this guy likes me!"

Yes, yes he did. Soon they had a date of sorts at a park, and he asked if he could kiss her. She thought "Uh oh—here we go, this could change everything." But it just so happened that an old couple was walking by holding hands, and Abby could suddenly see herself there, together with Martin in old age. Permission granted.

Some time later, he proposed to her at a railroad crossing (do these two know how to do symbolism, or what?). Undateable Martin turned out to be Marriageable Martin. Most of us tend to be impatient at railroad crossings, but not Abby—now, she gets to relive that happy moment over and over again.

Now back to parsing the question "Why should I settle?" The unspoken assumption seems to be that you somehow *deserve* somebody fabulous. But what does that mean? Does the person you have in mind even exist? Are they available to you? Will they be interested in you once you find them? These aren't easy questions to answer. In fact, they're not really the right questions. The right question is whether you can find somebody with character, with whom you have great rapport, who will make your life better in a big way? If you find such a person and have a happy life with them, you haven't settled. You've won.

EXPECTATIONS VS. ASPIRATIONS

Expect little, aspire to a lot.

Expectations are unnecessary limitations that you're placing on yourself. Life surprises us, and all sorts of good things can happen if we allow ourselves to go with the flow and stay open to possibilities. If you expect a certain kind of partner or relationship and are confronted with something different, you might miss out.

Aspirations, on the other hand, are perfectly reasonable. The trick is to aspire to the right thing. You can and should aspire to a great connection, and a great partnership. Just remember not to limit these aspirations by unreasonable expectations about particulars.

DATING AMBASSADORS

A friend of ours makes the great point that when you go out with someone for the first time, you're not really dating them—you're dating their ambassador. One doesn't need much experience in international politics to follow the analogy: the person you're going out with is trying to put their best foot forward, trying to create an impression, trying to finesse their way to the result they're looking for.

What often ensues is a sort of ritualized conversation in which one or both of you ask questions of each other according to formula: getting some background without getting too personal, making light-hearted banter which might or might not be actually amusing to either party, maybe sprinkling in a gentle compliment here or there.

This conversation is nothing at all like the conversation that the same two of you might have after you've gotten to know each other, and likely isn't even the same conversation that you'd have if you met as complete strangers, free of any romantic expectation.

That's not to say that the two of you are wrong for proceeding with your ambassadorial exchange—it's almost impossible not to. You'll get to know each other soon enough, and you'll relax, and you'll become fully yourselves.

The point isn't to nail the initial conversation; rather, it's almost the reverse. Don't worry too much about the initial conversation, and understand that however the other person is presenting themselves, it's probably not telling you all that much about who they are. Occasionally someone will be boorish enough at this stage that you're not much interested in spending any more time with them at all, but typically they'll be civil and possibly even charming, and it won't necessarily help you understand who they are.

YOUR PARTNER IS NOT YOUR POSSESSION

We talked earlier about the checklist—the one in which you look for a certain set of qualities and attributes in a potential partner—and why that might be a bad idea. Some people have the unfortunate habit of looking for a partner as if they're going shopping, and when they find the right one, they toss 'em in the cart. They've found someone, and now they move on to the next problem. Often, they proceed to treat their partner as just another acquisition, as just another possession.

Quick history refresher: we shit-canned slavery in this country a century and a half ago. We are now very clear on the legal point that one person cannot own another. Yet this sometimes breaks down in practice, especially in unhealthy relationships.

Part of the problem is these possessive pronouns that we insist on using when referring to each other: *your* boyfriend, *my* wife, *her* significant other. They create the illusion that our partners somehow belong to us, and many of us act that way. This sets up unrealistic expectations when it turns out that our partners are individuals in their own right, with their own expectations, their own aspirations, their own desires. When their world view or their actions don't perfectly align with our expectations of them, we can be frustrated, or disappointed, or even angry.

Your partner isn't yours; they're theirs. They're part of a two-person team, and so are you.

You don't have to do everything with your partner. For the vast majority of us, work will enforce a certain amount of separation, but a lot of people feel like they're supposed to spend most or all of their free time together.

When I was dating, I encountered someone online who looked like she might be interesting. She seemed interested in me, too, and we had just begun a pleasant correspondence when she discovered that I like to travel. And that was that. She didn't like to travel and felt that she couldn't be with anyone who did.

Of course, she might simply have been making an excuse— people do that all the time, especially on the low-commitment playing field of the Internet—but that didn't fit with the way the conversation had been going, and I had the impression that she was sincerely concerned about the travel issue. I never got the chance to find out what that was really about, whether it was a matter of taste, or an emotional block derived from a bad experience, or some medical/logistical issue. She was on to the next candidate, and I was left to keep looking.

The flaw in her reasoning was that if I traveled, she had to travel with me. I've traveled by myself many times, and while I sometimes might like the idea of my partner being by my side, it isn't strictly necessary for me to have a good time. I don't own my partner, nor does she own me. If Nancy has no interest in my next birding trip, or if I have no interest in going to the site of her next classroom gig, or if we simply have conflicts in our schedule, we can do our own thing. We always look forward to getting back together afterwards. (Which is invariably *really* nice, BTW.)

Not everything is an either/or proposition. Compromise is possible, whether it's about travel or anything else. You can play along in one situation that might be important to your partner, and they can play along for something that's important to you. The crucial thing here is that you're both invested in making each other happy, and that such compromises aren't unidirectional.

The two of you will be a team, and as you look for love, you should be keeping an eye out for somebody who will make a good teammate, somebody who will make your life better. That doesn't describe someone who wants to possess you and who wants to place limitations on you.

Some limitations are inevitable as you work out how you're going to function as a team. Most married couples and many committed couples pool their financial resources, most couples expect to be monogamous (though it's wise to be clear on this point), and there are limitations imposed by mutual decisions about having children, among many, many others.

The two important things are that you communicate and you don't place any limitations that aren't necessary to the function of the team. You've got to let your partner be themselves, consistently.

The point of this digression is that when you're looking for love, you're not looking for someone to fill a role for you. You're looking for a teammate, someone whose life you'll improve even as they're improving yours.

PEOPLE CHANGE...INCLUDING YOU

If you're really in this for the long haul, it's all the more important to find someone of character with whom you have a great rapport, because you'll (hopefully) have a long way to go. Several years from now you'll be a different person from the one you are now, and so will your partner. While it's a generally accepted truism that *you* can't change somebody, that doesn't mean *they* won't change—they'll just change in ways that you can't control. Their tastes might change in subtle ways, their perspective on life will almost certainly change, and circumstances might enforce a dramatic change. All of this can happen to you, as well. If you think back to who you were just a few years ago, I'll bet you can identify a couple of ways in which you've changed.

This is germane to dating. Consider the case of Sarah and Declan. They both think creatively when it comes to sex. They met at a "munch," which is a sort of social gathering for the kinkier crowd. It's not an orgy or even a sexual thing at all—it's just a bunch of open-minded people who like being around others who think like them. It was actually a fairly large gathering of maybe 60 people, just talking and hanging out in a local pizzeria. Because of the size of the group, Sarah and Declan almost didn't meet, but very near the end, they got into an intense conversation with a third person. Sparks started to fly, and they agreed to stay in touch.

They communicated back and forth and arranged to go to a pub night, as friends. Declan was to pick her up but got lost along the way. That didn't deter him, though, and at last he found her place. It was good that he didn't give up, because the sparks immediately started up again. They started driving, but they had to pull over to make out before they even got to the pub.

That was fun, but they were determined to carry on with their original plans for the evening. When they got inside, a little bit late (ahem), they found that the whole group had collected at one table. They had lost the game of musical chairs, and there were no seats left at the group table, so they sat at a side table.

They only knew one person in the place, a friend named Jeff who saw that they were sitting by themselves. He offered to join them until a thought struck him: "This isn't a *date*, is it?"

"No, no, no!" they both protested, and they insisted he join them. The three of them had a great time talking together, but when it was time to go home, it was just the two of them again. Cue sparks. Inevitably, they started making out again. (But it definitely wasn't a date.)

Whatever that meeting qualified as, they most certainly did start seeing each other. Along the way, Sarah made a discovery. Both of them like to experiment with dominance and submission. Both of them actually consider themselves switches, which means that they can play either the dominant or the submissive role. But both of them always had a clear preference for the dom side of things, and of the two of them, Declan was even a bit more of a

68

dom by nature. So Sarah rolled with that. She was used to guys falling in love with her, but she found herself falling in love with Declan. She felt a little bit out of control emotionally and likewise allowed herself to cede control to him in their sexual encounters.

To her surprise, she found she really liked that with Declan. She had always been the one in charge and had never thought she could make it work with a guy who was a dom. But at this stage in her life, she found that she was tired of being the one always in control. She has three kids, and her sister lives with her and relies upon her in a variety of ways. Even her parents turn to Sarah for advice.

It was a pleasant surprise to her when Declan took charge, and she found herself actively enjoying the loss of control. It worked for her because it was based on trust and mutual respect, which she expects from her lovers and which she gets from Declan, both in and out of the bedroom.

For his part, Declan was unemployed at the time and was in a different place in his life. His sexuality was the one area of his life in which he could be fully in control, and that definitely worked for him.

They are very much in love. They respect each other's character and have fantastic rapport. It works very well, but if Sarah had insisted on adhering to her traditional role, they might have had a hard time. She changed in a way that she was happy with, and it's possible that you'll find yourself changing when circumstances are right.

MAKE NO ASSUMPTIONS

Don't make assumptions about which type is or isn't right for
you. If we'd done that, Nancy and I might have missed out on
each other. For example, she used to think she didn't want someone who was athletic; I used to think I wanted someone who was.

Many people (such as Carla, who you'll meet later in the book)
are thrilled to find their twin, someone who acts like they do,
thinks like they do, has the same tastes and passions. But sometimes, as with Nancy and me, you don't need a twin.

Evie was going out with Josh, a good guy with whom she had
lots in common. Then one day her apartment was broken into
and robbed. She didn't lose too much of monetary value, but they
took her laptop, which had lots of stuff on it that hadn't been
backed up and that was meaningful to her on a personal level.
Worse than that was the feeling of violation, the sense that she
wasn't safe in her own apartment.

Evie describes herself as a bit on the neurotic side, prone to
drama and anxiety. So she reacted to the break-in exactly as she'd
expect: she freaked out. She immediately called Josh, looking
for support. But maybe she had a bit too much in common with
him: he reacted in much the same way she did. Instead of being
the calm, rational one that she needed in that moment, he freaked
out even more than she had. Of course that only magnified her
anxiety.

Eventually she moved through that incident and was able to put it
in perspective: it's an unfortunate truth that people get robbed all
the time, and although it was certainly unpleasant, the loss of her
laptop and a few other things didn't really cause that much harm.

She realized in the aftermath, however, that at least in some situations, she wanted someone who was different from her. Of course you can't judge an entire relationship on a single incident, but Evie became aware that she shouldn't assume that a kindred spirit would be what she wanted or needed in a partner.

The point is to be careful about making too many assumptions about "your type"—as you get to know someone, you'll come to understand whether that individual, regardless of type, is someone that you really connect with and really want to be with.

The other side of this coin is that you might assume that somebody isn't your type. Rochelle was a lesbian who hadn't had a really serious relationship. When she was 18 she met Andrew, and within the year they'd become the best of friends.

Because they were so close, it became an intimate relationship—including physical intimacy. But they never had intercourse, because—hey!—Rochelle was a lesbian! Within another year, they decided to move in together. And they regularly slept together. They crossed that last line, but still Rochelle self-identified as a lesbian. To the extent that, because they didn't want to have to explain themselves, they told friends that the guest bed was Andrew's bed. Note that Andrew never actually slept in Andrew's bed.

Rochelle could hardly pretend to herself that she wasn't into Andrew, including physically, so she started to describe herself as "lesbiandrew." She was still a lesbian, and he was simply a unique exception.

Eventually she went to work at a non-profit LGBT organization, and there she encountered a curious bias. The L's and the G's, it seemed, didn't think too much of the B's. It was as though bisexuals didn't share their problems, or that they were really just gays and lesbians in partial denial.

Rochelle bristled at that sort of thinking, and ultimately decided that she had to stand up for the bisexual community. She decided to identify as bisexual, in what she initially thought of as a political decision. She was addressing injustice. But once she stopped referring to herself as lesbian, or at least lesbiandrew, she realized that she really was, in fact, an honest-to-goodness bisexual. And she's now a happily-married-to-a-guy bisexual. Who knew?

Fortunately Rochelle is a very open-minded person, and her self-identification didn't keep her from partnering with Andrew in the first place. She figures that when you find the right person, you know it, and the labels begin to fall away.

That's a very clear and obvious case in which an assumption about your "type" could go astray. You might have assumptions that have nothing to do with your sexuality, but which nevertheless could keep you from giving someone a try, someone who might be terrific for you.

Of course, Rochelle is far from the only bisexual out there who needed a little while to sort out their sexuality. Linda started out identifying straight, as so many do. She met John, a guy she was attracted to. They married, and they made a great team, even founding a school together.

Linda and her husband had different styles, and they complemented each other, which helped them get things done. Unfortunately, their differences meant that they saw things differently, and they didn't always agree. Which is often fine.

Problem was, they both avoided conflict. They never fought, but it wasn't because they didn't have anything to fight about. They just didn't engage. Linda later heard from a friend that he never thought they'd last, because she was a passionate person and her husband was not. Whether or not his reasoning was correct, the result was the same.

Linda felt lost, and she had lost track of what she wanted and what she was good at; it was simpler to stay in a rut and do the same things over and over and avoid conflict in the process.

Of course that didn't work so well in the long run, and eventually they grew apart and divorced.

In the meantime, Linda had formed an intense friendship with a straight married woman named Susan. They'd spend an hour a day talking on the phone, and spent as much time together as they could. Eventually it got to a point where the Susan's husband decided they were spending *too* much time together, and he demanded that they cut off the relationship. Susan observed that she had never put that much energy into any relationship except her marriage.

Linda didn't get it, and couldn't understand why they couldn't continue to see each other.

Later Linda realized that she had been in love with Susan. She couldn't call it anything else. It wasn't a sexual thing, but it was real. But at the time, she hadn't put those words to it. As she put it: "The world wasn't in focus, and I didn't know why."

At about this same time, Linda, now single, was visiting with some dear friends, and somehow a discussion of sex got started. It seemed there was more than a little attraction between Linda and both halves of the couple she was visiting, and the evening ended up in a ménage à trois.

This was a watershed event for her. She enjoyed the guy half of the experience, but she found that she was *really* into the woman. And it was *definitely* a sexual thing.

The pendulum swung, and she interpreted this new development to mean that she was actually a lesbian. Long before she was confronted with the reality, she had speculated in her journal about whether she could possibly be a lesbian. Now she had evidence, and now she had a new way of self-identifying. At the age of 30, she came out. Turns out that everybody already knew it but her.

She never got to indulge her attraction for that first friend that she fell in love with, and the married friend she'd hooked up with wasn't available, but there were others out there.

Several years later she was working as a social worker at a VA hospital, and her manager Ted thought he saw in Linda a kindred spirit for another woman who had worked for him. He assumed they'd work as a couple because they were so similar. Ted asked Linda if she was interested in meeting someone. In principle, sure, but Linda balked when she heard the age difference: Margaret was seven years younger. Linda assumed that she'd be too immature.

As with many assumptions, there was a kernel of truth to this one. It wasn't really maturity per se—Linda agreed with Ted's assessment that Margaret was mature for her age—but the difference in years did manifest itself. There were things in Linda's past that, because of just a few years' frame of reference, weren't part of Margaret's past, and it was frustratingly difficult to talk about some things that were important to Linda.

This issue didn't prevent the relationship from flowering and lasting, however, and now they're married. Ted's partner, Stephen, also assumed that Linda and Margaret were going to work together, but he had entirely different reasoning from Ted: he viewed Linda and Margaret as opposites, and thought the yin/yang of their personalities would be the binding factor. However you slice it, it works.

That's not quite the end of the story, however. Linda sometimes reads lesbian erotica, but she often finds it lacking something. She was aware that she still liked the look of guys, she still fantasized about them, and if she was honest with herself, she still wanted them.

She'd long before come to understand that her assumption that she was straight wasn't correct. Now she understood that her assumption that she was strictly lesbian wasn't entirely correct, either. There was a name for what she is, and it's bisexual. It doesn't affect her marriage, but at least she finally understands who she is.

The moral of the story is to continually review your assumptions. Don't assume your way out of something great, and don't assume your way into something not-so-great.

BE READY TO MOVE ON

Dierdre lost the love of her life in a mountaineering accident. Jack was too young, and of course she never saw it coming. And that's germane: because he vanished from her life so quickly and without warning, she didn't have time to process it.

When you lose a partner during a break-up, you usually get it. You might have gotten ample warning that something was wrong with the relationship, but even if you didn't, the act of breaking up itself makes it pretty clear to you that you are now single.

It was different for Dierdre. She felt as though she were still married, but somehow her husband just wasn't around. Her focus was on her grief, not on her marital status. Consequently, it hadn't even occurred to her to look around.

A year before the accident, she had run into an old high school friend named Tim who had just lost his wife to cancer. Dierdre and Jack were solicitous of him and did what they could to comfort him in a series of conversations.

Then suddenly it was Dierdre's turn, and Tim got wind of it. He returned the favor. He'd had time to come to terms with his own tragedy, and now the focus was on Dierdre. They talked regularly, and he tried to be the best friend he could be. But there was a wrinkle: unbeknownst to her, Tim had had a crush on Dierdre back in high school, and he still had romantic feelings for her. Initially he tried to suppress these because that wasn't what Dierdre needed at the time, but as their friendship grew, he felt he had to reveal himself.

As the friendship had grown, Dierdre's opinion of Tim had grown, so though she hadn't been thinking in those terms, the idea of a romance with Tim was not at all unpleasant. Friendly conversations became romantic conversations, and eventually they both realized they'd found the second loves of their lives, and they're now each enjoying a second married life together.

Neither saw the other as a replacement for their spouse. Their original spouses couldn't be duplicated, of course, and since they'd had time to experience their friendship first, it was easy for them both to see that the other made life better in a different way. Not better than their original spouses, and not worse: just different.

Had the friendship not existed, the stakes might have seemed higher when they first met. It might have been frightening or uncomfortable, particularly in Dierdre's vulnerable state. And that would have interfered with them getting together.

If you've lost someone, regardless of circumstance, keep that point in mind: you're not trying to replace your previous partner. That's hard to do under any circumstances, but it's even harder if you had a terrific relationship. That's a tough act to follow, and it's damn near impossible to reproduce exactly.

You're not trying to do that. You're looking to start a new and different and rewarding relationship with someone else. If you come at it from that perspective, it's easier to be open to finding someone new. And if you're open to it, you have a better chance of success.

BE READY TO GAMBLE

If you offer to bet someone a quarter on something, they'll often refuse to bet on the grounds that they do not gamble. In their minds, it doesn't matter what the wager is about, and it doesn't matter how little the amount being wagered is. They simply do not gamble.

They are mistaken.

We *all* gamble, constantly. We gamble when we apply for a job. We gamble when we accept a job. We gamble when we go out in traffic that the other drivers will do the right thing (more or less).

We gamble when we go out with someone. We gamble when we get into a relationship.

All of that is good—taking chances is what enables us to lead a full and interesting life. The important thing is to make good gambles.

What does this mean for your love life? It means that you should be ready to consider your circumstances and make a leap of faith when the available evidence and your instincts tell you that you're with the right person. If it doesn't work out, at least you gave yourself a chance at having the sort of life you want to have.

Angus and Melanie did a little gambling. Melanie, who was living in Connecticut, had driven up to Boston for her college room-mate Audrey's bachelorette party.

Angus was over from Scotland on a soccer tour, playing with a club team of alumni from his alma mater.

The team went out one night, but they encountered an obstacle: they couldn't reach the bar because Melanie and her friends were in their way.

There was only one thing to be done, and that was to engage the obstacle head-on. Commence banter, commence flirtation. Commence Angus meeting Melanie. The guys and gals spent the whole night dancing together and even had breakfast together the next morning. Angus and Melanie clicked in a big way.

Just one problem: the 3000+ miles between Hartford, Connecticut and Edinburgh, Scotland.

Problems can be overcome, however. Perhaps it was shrewd judgment, perhaps it was a bit of alcohol, perhaps it was both, but

Audrey could see the connection between Angus and Melanie, and she invited Angus to her wedding as Melanie's date.

The team was still going to be in the States for another week, and Angus, who knew he was on to something good, made the most of it. He made arrangements to see Melanie a couple more times, even skipping a game to see her one last time before flying home. He was already gambling that this was going to work out.

Of course Angus's soccer team was keenly aware of all of this, and they did a bit of gambling themselves: they took bets with each other on whether this whirlwind romance was going to work out.

By the time he headed home, Angus had all the information he needed to make his bet: he was, in fact, going to get on a plane in three weeks and show up for Audrey's wedding.

So he did, and the fates seemed to be intervening to make it all go smoothly. He was supposed to hop a bus from Logan Airport in Boston up to the wedding in New Hampshire, but as luck would have it, the pilot on the flight from Glasgow recognized him out on the curb, and discovered that they were heading in the same direction. He gave Angus a ride curb-to-curb, no bus required.

Angus and Melanie had a great time at Audrey's wedding, and they were committed. They both had jobs that paid well, so they could afford to buy airline tickets, and took turns flying to see each other every couple of weeks.

Now it was Melanie's turn to gamble: they wanted to close that 3000-mile gap, and she reasoned that Edinburgh was a more interesting city than Hartford, so she moved all the way to Scotland to be with Angus.

They married within a couple of years, and decided to raise a family in the U.S. So they gambled again. They made arrangements to stay with Audrey while they looked around for a place to live, and on the drive up to New Hampshire, they drove through Melrose, MA, and were charmed. They decided right then and there that they wanted to live in Melrose, and they've lived there happily ever since, raising their two children, the second of which is named after that bar where they made their first gamble.

The trick is to understand when the rewards outweigh the risks, and when a gamble with your heart is the only rational move to make.

GREED IS BAD, EXCEPT WHEN IT'S GOOD

Money matters. So whatever you do, know what you do and don't need. It's very romantic to think that love conquers all. Sometimes it really does. In lots and lots and lots of other cases, however, mismatches between expectations and financial realities put a big strain on relationships.

The important thing is to make sure that you're going to have enough money. If your tastes are simple and you and your prospective partner are both responsible people, you have a chance to be very happy together. If one of you is irresponsible, however, you can easily imagine getting into the kind of trouble that strains a relationship to the breaking point.

Money is usually a nice-to-have. Disposable income is a good thing—you can go places and do things that might not otherwise be available to you. You're in position to lend a hand to your friends and family, or maybe throw a few bucks to charity. Still, for some people too much of a good thing is not a good thing.

I have two good friends who decided that the guys they were dating had *too much* money—they didn't think they shared the same values, and each of them feared a power mismatch in their relationships.

Not that financial mismatches can't work—of course they can. There are all sorts of things that one can bring to a relationship. Just because you don't have as much money as your partner doesn't mean you won't make their life better each and every day.

Money is a practical issue; it's an enabler. Focus on what you're really after—the happiness that can come through genuine love—and make sure that whatever you do gets you closer to that goal.

CHAPTER 3
PLAN BE

Plan A is to find the right partner. Plan Be is to enjoy your life regardless. Alphabetization aside, Plan Be should come first.

Not everyone has the good fortune to find a great partner, and it's important to remember that it's better to be single than to be with the wrong partner.

Regardless of your relationship status, your first order of business is to like who you are and to live the sort of life you want to live. If you do those things, you'll be having fun, and you'll seem like fun to others. You'll be more likely to exude confidence and relaxation—and people will take away a favorable impression of you. And maybe want to see more of you.

All of that is easy enough to say, of course, but perhaps not so easy to put in practice. Still, it's important to keep in mind. Much has been written about how to be who you want to be, and that's not the focus of this book, but it's something to pay attention to even as you look outside yourself for that great partner.

BE HAPPY WITH YOURSELF

This actually shows up a bit late in the book, given how important it is. Try this on: *you're at your most attractive when you're happiest with yourself.*

Doesn't that sound right? Obvious, almost? OK, maybe you're thinking "I won't be happiest with myself until I find my someone." But keep Plan Be in mind. You have to like you. Warts and all.

Maybe you don't like your job, or you'd like to lose a few pounds, or you've done something you're not proud of. You are who you are, and at some point you need to strike a balance between self-improvement and self-acceptance.

Many people are much harder on themselves than anyone around them is. I had a client who was a standout athlete in high school, got into and graduated from one of the most selective universities in the country, did well in business before following her dream of being a writer, and published several critically acclaimed books with a major publishing house. Oh, and just to round it all out, she has a loving husband and three terrific kids. It's the sort of cloying American-dream existence that others envy. Yet she imagined herself to be some sort of failure, because she had left the business world behind, and her books weren't selling at Rowling-esque levels.

Clearly, perspective matters.

We might not all have the dazzling resume that my client has, but we each have something to offer. We can all exist well in the world, being kind to ourselves and to others. To the extent that we can let go of expectations, both internal and external, we can be our best selves.

In some ways it hardly matters what collection of circumstances and traits you have. What mistakes you've made, or what flaws you perceive in yourself. Because you are who you are, and these are the cards you've been dealt. There's a best way to play this hand, and you've got to figure it out.

Coming to terms with who you are is your first priority. Once you've done that, even if you're still actively making changes in your life, you'll be ready to meet the right person.

DO THE STUFF YOU LOVE

Our friend Steve tells the story of a college friend who tried to fix him up with his sister's best friend Libby one weekend. Problem was that Steve already had plans. He loved classical music and had been looking forward to attending a concert at Tanglewood, a famous local musical venue. The concert was important to him.

He said to his friend "Fine, but I'm going to Tanglewood this weekend. If she wants to go along, that's great."

It was fine. Arrangements were made, and they went off and had a really fun weekend enjoying the music and spending time together. Libby got to see Steve being fully himself. They had a wonderful time that weekend, and ultimately they fell in love and got married. They continue to have a wonderful time together, being themselves.

Another friend is a classic bird watching geek. He was out at a bar one night, and when the girl next to him mentioned something about a mockingbird in conversation with a friend, he overheard it, and he promptly rattled off its Latin name: "Oh, you mean Mimus polyglottos!".

If you're looking for dating tips, that one isn't high on the list of recommended pick-up lines. Which is actually an advantage in many circumstances. He was simply being himself, and wasn't pretending to be anything else. His geeky conversational gambit was just the thing to spark a conversation: she shared his interest in birds, and they set up a date to go birding the next morning, and so began a romance leading to a long and happy marriage.

A couple of chapters ago I told you about Mike. He was just doing what he does, water-skiing and relaxing, and he got to be his best self. He socialized, he helped out and acted the hero, and his skiing skills probably didn't make him any less attractive, either. Even if he hadn't met his future wife that way, he was doing something he loved, and his life was that much better for having done it.

You can live your life that way, too. It might not be water-skiing, and it might not be recreation at all. You can spend much of your time in a job you love, or simply being in the presence of friends or family, even as you look for opportunities to meet someone. The point is to make sure that you're enjoying your life *now*, not just waiting for some vague point in the murky future.

> **THOUGHT EXPERIMENT**: When do you feel like you're at your very best, and most appealing to other people? Wouldn't it be nice if a really interesting person saw you being that way? How can you make that happen more often?

SEE THE BIG PICTURE

Planning ahead can go a long, long way toward enjoying your life. Sure, there are times you want to live in the moment, and that's important, but when figuring out how to conduct your life, you should be prepared in case you're going to live it without a partner.

Gina learned about divorce at a young age. Her parents divorced, and she saw how her mother struggled financially. She could imagine the same thing happening to her one day, so she wanted to be ready when it did. She wanted to get married, but actually thought she'd probably get divorced eventually, and it was her plan to be financially independent when that happened.

The next step for Gina was to figure out how she wanted to make that happen. In college, she gravitated toward accounting. She liked the subject, and it came naturally to her. In her words, "I could smoke pot, drink, do cocaine, and still get an A." While I wouldn't recommend that program for figuring out what you want to do, Gina could see that accounting worked perfectly for her——she considers herself a very black-and-white person, and reconciling the books felt ideal to her.

Eventually she slowed down her lifestyle and started a career in accounting. She had a Plan Be; she could support herself. But she met a guy, and he seemed just right for her, too. She got married, had two kids...and found out that she didn't need that divorce after all.

Plan A worked, and she didn't need her Plan Be. She's the CFO of a small company, and she loves her job—agreeable work, great colleagues, even an easy commute. And she's the primary breadwinner in the household. So she'd be all set if she needed to go it alone.

But she doesn't.

ENJOY THOSE OTHER RELATIONSHIPS

The primary focus of this book is finding love, specifically in the context of a long-term relationship. But just as love matters, those other relationships matter as well.

Your family relationships are important, of course, and your relationships with your old friends are important as well. But you can always find new friends, in many forms.

Here are some different kinds of relationships that you can enjoy, many of which might develop with people who you've connected with as you search for romance:

THE PLATONIC FRIEND	This is the friend with whom things never quite clicked romantically, or who you got to know just as a friend and romance was never on the table. Pretty much like any good friend, only this person happens to be of the gender you're interested in romantically. The trick is to make sure that both of you are on the same page about what this friendship is, especially if there are unrequited feelings.
THE ACTIVITY FRIENDSHIP	This might or might not be a deep friendship, but there's someone who you really enjoy doing a specific activity with. I have female friends who I enjoy birding with, for example, and you might know somebody you can call if e.g. you want to see a concert or scour the local antique shops.
THE FLING	While waiting to find your keeper, you might have a brief but exciting romantic relationship with someone. Maybe it's when you're traveling, or maybe it's at home, but you know it's going to be temporary. As long as nobody is misrepresenting what's going on, this can be a lot of fun in the short term.

THE FRIEND WITH BENEFITS	This might be longer term than the fling, but again, there's no intention of long-term romance; it's simply about an enjoyable sex life, even in the absence of a long-term relationship.
THE WORK SPOUSE	Sometimes you can have a close friendship with someone who's unavailable. One of the common scenarios is a co-worker whom you like and respect, and with whom you spend a great deal of time. This can be rewarding as long as boundaries are honored.
THE EX-LOVER	It's possible to love someone who you can't live with. One or both of you might realize that you can't make this relationship work in terms of a long-term partnership, but that doesn't mean you can't be dear friends, and can't enrich each other's lives.
THE NON-SEXUAL PARTNER	Just as it's possible to love someone you can't live with, it's also possible to live with someone you don't love. This might be someone who's the perfectly compatible housemate for you, and you might even vacation together, sharing costs along the way.

These are just some examples; you can probably think of others. The point is that, as you search for love, it can be worthwhile to be open to any number of different relationships that will enrich your life.

CHAPTER 4

SCREW THE DATE; JUST RELATE

All right, you've got your motivation, you know what you're looking for, you have your Plan Be. Now it's time to put Plan A into effect. Now that you know what you want and you're ready to date, don't worry about dating. Worry only about connecting. Many of those meetings might take the *form* of a date, and that's fine. It can be a cup of coffee, or dinner and a movie, or a shared activity, or just conversation at a laundromat.

The point is not to think of it as a romantic encounter with your future love. Which isn't to say that it might not turn into that—hey, why not? Might as well shortcut the process if you can. Nancy was my 69th date, but I was just her 4th! But don't assume that it's going to happen quickly, and don't sweat it if it doesn't. You're just getting to know each other. Take the pressure off yourself--and take it off whomever you're with while you're at it.

Each meeting is potentially the start of a relationship, which can mean lots of different things. The interaction might go no further than the first get-together, so that's a pretty limited sort of relationship. Subsequent meetings might lead to a friendly acquaintance, a business relationship, a deep friendship, a failed romance, a successful-for-a-while romance, a serious long-term relationship, or even marriage. Or none of the above. It's possible that you'll have a meeting with this person in one context and then encounter them in an entirely different context a few weeks later.

You just don't know. And because you don't know, you should give the person the benefit of the doubt and treat them with respect and kindness, the way you would treat anyone. That should go without saying, but when some people are sizing up a potential love interest, they can be hypercritical and sometimes even downright rude, as if they were thinking "No way I'd ever marry someone like *you!*"

The person you're meeting with might not have read this book. They might be investing too heavily in this date and consequently putting too much pressure on it. That will make it harder for you, of course, but you can affect the equation by taking the pressure off of it yourself.

We're better than we sometimes realize at reading each other's body language and picking up on unspoken signals. If you convey the sense that you're at ease, you might put them at ease, which might let a little more air in to the room, and give your budding connection a chance to breathe a little.

You also might just raise the issue and point out that people often put too much pressure on a date. You might even suggest a two-date minimum, the way Nick did earlier in the book.

Consider Virginia and Al. They traveled in similar circles in college and knew each other, but not well. After college they ended up in different places: she went to DC, and he moved to Boston. Eventually, he traveled down to Washington to visit friends and once again crossed paths with Virginia. Taking advantage of the opportunity, he asked her out, and she accepted.

He allowed her to pick the place, and she chose a very nice Asian fusion restaurant. First date, expensive place: a good recipe for discomfort. Al seemed quiet and ill at ease in the fancy restaurant. He was out of his element. The conversation lagged, and Virginia began to conclude that he was kind of boring. She had a different kind of guy in mind: an alpha male who would be confident, take charge, pursue her aggressively, and generally act like he owned the place. Al was different, and in the moment, that didn't seem like a good thing.

But Al was Al, and after he'd returned to Boston, he called her. And he called her again. And kept calling her with what she called "passive-aggressive persistence." She was coming to realize that he was a genuinely nice guy who actually *did* have a sort of quiet confidence, the kind of confidence that was not going to be easily dissuaded in pursuit of her. By the time he sent her roses for Valentine's Day, she was sold. Now she thinks of Al as "the most comfortable-in-his-skin person I've ever met." Not at all the impression she formed in their high-pressure, nice-restaurant first date.

But it isn't just about the meeting. It's about the mindset. It's about your approach to meeting people generally. Screw the date —just see how you can relate to the people you're connecting with, and see where it goes.

REFRAME THE GAME: HAVE A PLEASANT TIME

OK, we know that your overall goal is to find a partner. So it's natural that when you go on a date, you think your goal is to find a partner. *But that shouldn't be your primary goal.* If you're out on a date, you've already found a candidate. *Now* your goal is to have a pleasant outing, and see what sort of relationship might or might not develop with this person.

Whatever that might be is probably not going to be decided in one encounter, so there's no reason to rush things. Instead, be yourself and have a good time.

Here are a few ideas for having a good date.

- *Be curious.* Find out who this person is and what's interesting about them. Understand them, get their backstory. Learn, both about them and about yourself. Through various women I dated I was exposed to some art forms I hadn't previously appreciated, learned some interesting stuff about human vision, and even improved my Spanish. Among other things.

- *Be open to new experiences.* Have a good time at the meeting. You don't have to be passive. If you want to be sure to have fun, come up with an idea that would be fun for you. I once met a woman for the first time at a cemetery in Cambridge, Massachusetts, not far from where she lived. Mount Auburn Cemetery was founded in 1831 as the first garden cemetery in the United States. It's a beautiful place, and it has a lot of interesting people buried there, such as Henry Wadsworth Longfellow, Mary Baker Eddy, and Winslow Homer, just to name a few. A cemetery might not seem like the most sensible place for a first date, but it was great. There was no romantic connection, as it happened, but we had a really good time looking at all of the gravestones and imagining all of the stories behind them. Regardless of the outcome, a long walk on a nice day in an interesting setting was a pleasant way to pass the morning.

And probably a better time than a typical dinner at a typical restaurant would have been.

- *Let go of the expectations.* There's nothing to fear from a date or any other meeting if you're not too invested in the outcome. You can simply have a nice time. Or maybe not, but if you don't expect anything, no real harm done. Other good stuff can happen: you can meet a life-long friend or maybe the person who will one day introduce you to the love of your life. And if you're not worried about the outcome, something romantic just might happen.

A perfect example is Leanne. She and her friend were both single, and Leanne was well familiar with her friend Sheri dragging her out to something or another and then abandoning her once they were out. So when Sheri started bugging her about going on a harbor cruise, Leanne resisted. For a solid week Sheri kept bugging her about and making promises that this time would be different, and finally Leanne caved. Off they went and, true to form, within half an hour Sheri had abandoned her.

Leanne was furious. So when Paul showed up, asking her to dance and chatting her up, Leanne wasn't really focused on the guy in front of her. As a result, she wasn't the least bit nervous, as she might have been under other circumstances. Instead she was just herself. Leanne didn't attach any meaning to the fact that Paul was chatting her up, and when at the end of the cruise he asked if he could call her, it somehow didn't occur to her that he had romantic intentions. She'd made no effort to impress Paul, and paradoxically (or maybe not), he was impressed. Meeting a guy on a harbor cruise might have been fraught with expectation, but not for Leanne, and something good was able to come out of it as a result.

- *Get a new story out of each encounter.* Every interaction is a part of your narrative arc. Your story might have more or less drama than someone else's, but it's yours, and you might as well make the best of it. We love a good story. You can get a lot of mileage out of even the most awkward encounter (raise your hand if you've repeated a bad date story more than once). I like to remind myself that when things go wrong in ways that don't have serious consequences, the value of the story often exceeds the discomfort in the moment. And eventually, you can tell a happy tale, one of the sort of tale that's sprinkled throughout this book.

You might have different ideas for how to have a good date. The details aren't what matters; it's the approach. Enjoy yourself.

SLOW AND STEADY WINS THE RACE

We all know the expression "slow and steady wins the race," and we all know what it means, but a lot of us never quite get around to remembering that lesson everywhere it applies. Dating is one of those places.

Have you ever resolved that you'd get yourself out there, then gone on a bunch of dates, tried really hard, gotten disappointed, and then bailed out for a week, a month, or a year or three? Good for you if you haven't, but lots of people do exactly that. Since you now already kinda/sorta know the odds are slim that your beloved is going to waltz into your life in the next day or two, you're going to want to pace yourself. Pace yourself so you'll be consistent, so you'll be diligent. So that chance you give yourself this week will be followed by another chance next week, and the week after that, and for as many weeks as it takes until—*voilà!*—no more chances required.

What does this mean? It means knowing yourself. Know how much energy you have, how much time you have, how much of this stuff you can handle. Plan ahead for what your run rate might look like—how many people are you going to connect with over the course of a typical month?

Getting myself out there wasn't much of a problem for an extroverted guy like me. If I went out with someone and the date was a dud, I rarely considered it time poorly spent. I just considered it to be part of the cost of doing business. Not that I was always so cool about it in the moment if things didn't work out, but I was usually able to put things in perspective after the initial disappointment.

I really had no problem with frequent one-time dates, but you might not be like me. Maybe you're very introverted and going out is a serious chore for you. Maybe you're exhausted even after a great date. Maybe you don't have the time to go out every week. That's fine. Work within your own limitations. If it's a bit tougher for you, so be it, but that doesn't mean you shouldn't try. You're playing to win—do whatever gives you your best chance. If that's means you only go out once every other week, or even once a month, so be it. Just be clear about what you're up for, and give yourself your best chance by running a slow, steady race. The more people you meet, the more you connect with, the more you flirt with, and the more you discuss your love life with, the better your odds are. You're optimizing for yourself, not anybody else.

Becca optimized for herself. She's very shy and introverted, and she had never really dated. But she's smart and good-looking, and guys noticed. When she was in her teens and twenties, there always seemed to be a friend around who would eventually blossom into a romance, so she didn't lack for relationships.

When she found herself single again in her 30s, there just weren't as many opportunities for her to meet interesting guys. Additionally, there had been a fair amount of ambiguity about where her last relationship was going and how serious it was, and she didn't want that.

She decided to try online dating, where at least (as she thought) most people were being clear about their intentions. She learned that wasn't always the case; e.g. some guys clearly just wanted to hook up but didn't say so in their profile. So she still dreaded the thought of dating, but she made it work for her.

Becca wasn't in a rush to get into just any old romance. She took her time to try to get in the *right* romance. And she did it in a way that wasn't too draining for her. She engaged in a series of rather long correspondences with guys she met online, to suss out their expectations and minimize the actual dates.

Others can tell you that this doesn't always work—someone you correspond with online can often seem very different from the one you meet in person—and to be sure, Becca wasn't meeting many guys doing it her way. But it worked for her in that she was able to keep doing it.

When I say that she wasn't meeting many guys, I understate the case. For a long time she didn't even meet a single guy in person this way. But after one of those long correspondences with a guy named Justin, she felt a comfort level she hadn't felt before. He was the first guy she agreed to meet with.

It worked out marvelously well for her. Becca and Justin completely clicked at that meeting, started seeing each other, and have been in a committed relationship ever since.

So she's found the happy ending and still hasn't really dated. Not bad, eh? Individual results may vary, of course. Becca is an extreme case, and I offer you her story not as a template for you to follow, but to make the point that even her slow, cautious methodology gave her the chance to succeed because she was able to stick with it.

If you meet a few or a lot more potential partners over time than Becca did, your odds improve accordingly. Her story is a useful reminder that there is more than one way to go about finding love, and if you find a way that you can sustain, you give yourself your best chance.

DOESN'T MATTER HOW, DOESN'T MATTER WHERE, DOESN'T MATTER WHEN

More than once, I told someone how I met Nancy through online dating, and they responded with something like "I want it to be more romantic than that." But let's think this one through. They're going to run the risk of not meeting a great partner solely to preserve a slim chance that they'll find another one according to some vague script? Nancy and I got off to an unromantic start, but hey, we had a honeymoon in Paris. Which was pretty damn good, actually. It goes without saying that having a romance is *waaay* more romantic than not having a romance. So please don't sweat the how.

Likewise, it doesn't matter *where* you meet the love of your life. When I talked to Nancy on the phone for the first time, she said something about dropping her sister off at the airport the next morning. It just so happened that I was flying out to Seattle the next day, so I quickly suggested we could meet at the airport. That evening, I told a friend about it, and she vehemently asserted that I couldn't possibly meet someone at the airport and what the hell was wrong with me anyway, or words to that effect.

I wasn't buying it, and we'd already set things up anyway. So despite my friend's well intentioned advice, Nancy and I went ahead with our meeting, as planned. Our romantic meeting place was at the top of the escalator in Terminal C at Logan Airport. We looked around for the nearest place that sold coffee—a McDonald's in the food court, as it happened—and immediately started hitting it off. We were completely at ease with each other right from the start. If anything, I'd figure that the casual setting only helped, but I imagine that our first meeting would have gone wonderfully well no matter where we met. Nancy isn't sure, though, that had we been in a more romantic setting, she would have been as comfortable and as much herself.

But it's not just us, and the airport isn't the only off-beat venue where you can find love. Pam was driving home on the turnpike in western Massachusetts one day, and there weren't many cars on the road. In fact there seemed to be just her and a blue Saturn, and the two of them were taking turns passing and following, following and passing. Just some guy. Kinda cute, about her age. Just saying. Soon it seemed they were developing a rhythm in their driving, and then—why not?—they started improvising, swapping lanes in synchrony and doing whatever else occurred to them to alleviate the boredom. By this time they were grinning at each other as they passed. One could even say they were flirting. Of course, we all know that you don't meet up with perfect strangers on highways (right?), and eventually their paths diverged, and that was that. Pam sure had enjoyed the flirting, though, and couldn't help but wonder about the what-ifs....

So life went on, and a few weeks later, a funny thing happened. Pam once again found herself driving on that same stretch of the Mass Pike, and—what do you know?—there was that same blue Saturn, driven by that same cute guy! This fact escaped neither of them, and their smiles told each other all they needed to know. He gave her the universal sign for drinking a cup of coffee, and at the next exit they pulled over to grab a cup and actually talk to each other. And actually get to know each other. And then, yes... of course they ended up getting married.

It is possible to find love even in places that are the antithesis of romantic.

Liza and Devin knew each other in college—they lived in the same dorm. College, of course, offers a wide array of single people from which to choose, and many of those people are rather attractive. Liza never gave Devin a second look. He was kind of a geeky kid, and, well, Liza's hormones suggested to her that she should be more interested in those big, hunky jock types.

Off they went on their separate ways into the world, and several years later, now in their 30s, they got the sad news that their beloved residence director, Sally, had died young after a battle with cancer.

At the memorial service, there wasn't a great deal of social interaction, but Devin lived nearby and thought that several of the old friends should get together and revisit shared memories of Sally.

So he invited the gang to go over to his place, and Liza was happy to join them.

This second gathering was more upbeat, with drinks, with laughter, with long conversations. Devin and Liza engaged in one of these conversations, and with it came flirtation. Rather a lot, actually. When things started to break up, Devin asked Liza out, and she readily accepted.

As they got to know each other, Liza could see that Devin was a solid, steady, responsible guy, and they had a lot of shared tastes, and suddenly she didn't need to worry about how buff he was or how good at sports he might have been. This was a man of substance, and she found herself falling in love with him.

The two of them think that Sally would have loved the fact that they got together at her memorial service. Liza has a friend who similarly met her husband at a funeral, and they like to joke that it's the best place to meet guys, despite the somber occasion—lots of people thrown together through mutual affection, and nobody's feeling any pressure because of the setting.

Whether or not that's true, it is unquestionably the case that some pretty offbeat settings can be the catalysts for finding love, if you're open to it.

THOUGHT EXPERIMENT: Can you imagine yourself in a thoroughly unromantic setting, walking up to someone who looks like they might have potential, and saying hello? The extroverts are shrugging—sure, I guess—as the introverts are vigorously shaking their heads no. Fair enough, introverts, but go ahead and imagine it anyway. Of course you have to make some conversation about something, and of course there's always the threat of awkwardness, but somebody a very long time ago pointed out that nothing ventured is nothing gained. Again, you don't have to treat this person as anyone special. You're just making conversation, connecting in a small way, and just maybe sparking something that will lead one of you to get back in touch with the other. In fact it doesn't have to be a romantic possibility at all. It could be someone of any age or gender. In the meantime you'll get practice at making connections, and over time you'll become more at ease with it. And the more times you do it, and the easier it gets, the better the chances that you'll really connect in a meaningful way with someone...

MAKE IT EASY FOR YOURSELF

A point related to the doesn't-matter-how/when/where approach is that whatever you do, you should feel at ease.

Part of the point of taking the pressure off the date is that you want to be relaxed and fully yourself. One way to do this is to simply not worry about how, or where, or when. But what if you're not quite that Zen, and you're going to worry anyway?

The fact that you're trying to connect with someone authentically doesn't mean that you're unaware of the romantic potential. The fact that you're not taking this meeting too seriously doesn't mean that you aren't hoping that something will click. It's human nature to want to put your best foot forward. You can still make choices about the circumstances of your meeting, as long as the process of creating those circumstances doesn't become too stressful.

Maybe you'd prefer to meet someone in a setting where you feel relaxed, like your favorite coffee shop. Or maybe you can't quite help worrying about your appearance, and you'd rather meet in a place where you like the lighting.

All of that is fair enough. The larger point is to be at ease. Don't invest *too* much effort in the perfect place, don't be *too* particular about the setting, be as flexible as you can without feeling uncomfortable. But whatever you do, make it work for you.

GO TRADITIONAL *IF* IT WORKS FOR YOU

We've talked about lots of alternatives to the classic dinner date. Those are great if they help you take the pressure off and connect with someone in a healthy way.

That's not to say that you can't go on a traditional sort of date. You absolutely can, if that's what works for you.

Some people like a dinner date. Maybe it's the one time all week you'll get to go out. Maybe you work in a casual setting, and you relish the chance to dress up and look sharp. Maybe you like a good meal and are tired of cooking the same old things over and over again.

Regardless of the approach you take, it's incumbent on you to keep things in perspective, to not put any pressure on the situation, and to do your best to take the pressure off the person you're with. Know yourself. And make your best guess about the person you're with. Whatever maximizes the fun for both of you, whatever gives you the best chance to get to know each other and connect with each other authentically—that's exactly what you should be doing.

LET THE CONNECTION DETERMINE THE PERSON

That rapport stuff we talked about earlier leads me to a useful strategy: the surest way for you to find a great partner is to wait until you feel a genuine connection with someone, rather than trying to force a connection that doesn't really exist with someone who appeals to you in some way.

Let me give you an example. Let's say that Person A is a bona fide hottie and admirable in various ways. You're fascinated by Person A. But when you talk to Person A, the conversation is awkward, you're looking for something to talk about, and while you enjoy the buzz of being in Person A's presence, you don't really have that great a time, and neither does Person A. But since you're fascinated, you persist. Nothing good results. Surprise, surprise.

Then you bump into Person B, who you'd barely noticed before. Laughs, mutual understanding, fun, and a desire to hang around with Person B that's quite independent of Person B's resume.

Who is likely to be a better choice for you? Of course you know. As desirable as Person A seems, you belong with someone like Person B. In the first case, you were letting the person determine the connection. In the second, you were letting the connection determine the person.

Betsy had dated all throughout college, and continued dating after college. Her thoughts about the various guys she dated were things like "he's nice" or "it could work." Not inspiring stuff. Fortunately she possessed enough self-awareness to understand that none of them were quite right for her. She did meet one guy that she thought she was kind of into, but he literally moved to the end of the earth, going to Antarctica to realize a long-sought after opportunity to further his career as a physicist.

When her friend Margot came to visit her in Boston, Betsy was in the middle of a move and had very little free time. Margot also wanted to catch up with Ian, an old high school friend, so with Betsy's permission, she killed two birds with one stone and invited Ian to visit with her while she helped Betsy pack.

The three of them had a great time hanging out together and bantering as they packed, and Betsy couldn't remember when she had laughed so much. She and Ian immediately felt at ease with each other. When the work was done, they agreed to stay in touch. Betsy had just bought a new phone, and Ian punched his name into her phone for her as "Ian (Margot's friend)."

Not long after that, Betsy called Ian (Margot's friend), and he soon became Ian (Betsy's friend). Though they both started out with friendship in mind, their obvious connection asserted itself, and before very long at all, a mutual romantic interest became clear to both of them.

They started seeing each other, and eventually they moved in together. No chasing, no seduction, just a fundamental connection. They communicate wonderfully well, and have a drama-free relationship. In the absence of game-playing, it had a great chance from the very start, and they're now enjoying the results.

NO, REALLY: IT'S NOT ABOUT THE DATE

Ever gotten your hopes up about a date? Maybe this time? You almost can't help having expectations. And the higher those expectations, the more likely you are to find yourself disappointed.

Sometimes those expectations are about the trappings of the date: are we going to the right restaurant, is the food good there, are we both looking good?

Not the stuff you need to care about. Those things don't matter in the slightest in the end. Maybe they're nice to have for atmosphere, sure, but what really counts is the connection that you make or don't make, regardless of what sort of date it is. Forgive me for belaboring this point, but it's important.

When Renee was a freshman in college, Aaron was a friend of some of her classmates, and they got to know each other. Eventually he asked her out, and she was happy to accept.

Renee assumed that he had specific plans in mind for the evening, but he didn't. They ended up just going for a drive from Haverhill, MA to Ogunquit, ME and back.

On the way back to her dorm he got pulled over for tailgating the car in front of them (according to the police officer). Aaron had to turn off the amp under his seat so it didn't drain his battery, but that action made one of the officers suspicious, so he pulled Aaron out and searched the car. Renee was in the front passenger seat with Dunkin' Donuts trash above her ankles—apparently it hadn't occurred to him to clean out his car before a first date.

One of the cops shined a flashlight in Renee's eyes while Aaron was being searched. The cop asked her if there was anything in the car that she should be aware of, and she said "I haven't a clue;

this is our first date." The cop then asked her to kick around the trash by her feet, and she asked: "Do I have to? I'm afraid of what I might get stuck with." The cop laughed and asked her if there was going to be a second date. She said it wasn't looking good.

At the time, she had no plans of ever going out with him again because of the messy car, the lack of plans, and the fact that they got pulled over. I'll let her tell the rest:

> *They let him go with a warning and when he got back in the car and pulled away he looked at me with this glimmer in his eyes and said "At least we have a good first date story for years to come." That look in his eye, and the fact that he was already thinking long term even though we hadn't done anything that night besides just talk, got him a second date. I still have to deal with trash on the passenger side floor of his car to this day, but every time I have to kick it aside I think of that first date and still get butterflies.*

When Alec was dating his wife, he went one step further with the law. Patricia was subletting the apartment above him in Boston one summer, and they hit it off pretty quickly. They began dating, and she invited him to a semi-formal dance at Curry College, where she was a student (he went to Boston University). He'd been hanging out with his buddies, and they were all having a beer. But now Patricia was ready to go, and they all went to the car with their beers in their hands. As it happened, a police cruiser was rolling by at that moment, and one of the cops saw his friend getting into the car with a beer in his hand. Alec watched and, while his friend was being handcuffed, he discreetly hid his own beer behind his foot. Just as he was about to leave, his beer tipped over, and he was busted, too. The cop hauled the three of them in, and while they were spending a couple of hours in a holding cell, Patricia and their other roommate were busy arranging to bail them out.

Eventually they were sprung, and Alec and Patricia hurried down to Curry. They arrived at the dance at 10 pm, an hour before it ended. It would have been really easy for Patricia to be frustrated and furious with Alec for spoiling their evening, but she had a much healthier approach: she was amused by the entire thing and rather proud that she'd bailed him out, and she had a great time regaling her friends with the story.

She knew that Alec wasn't trouble—this was his one and only run-in with the police—so she didn't take the incident seriously. Instead she took what could have been a disastrous date and made it into one of their favorite old stories.

These may seem like two lousy dates on paper, but they led to great things. You really can't get much clearer than that: it's not about the date, it's about the connection.

Conversely, there are many times people have unrealistic expectations of what a successful date should look like. That's a set-up for disappointment, because there are any number of reasons that a date might not succeed.

WHEN BAD DATES HAPPEN TO GOOD PEOPLE

We all know about bad dates. Some people use them as evidence that dating sucks, or that their romantic luck is horrible. But bad dates can happen to anybody, and they're part of the equation. You just have to assume that they're coming, wait for them to pass, and be ready for the good dates.

There are lots of ways that things can go awry on a date:

- *Zero chemistry.* Ideally this is mutual, but sometimes it's one-sided. Sigh.

- *A bad day.* Somebody might be physically unwell, but they don't say anything. They just don't impress anybody in that condition. Or maybe there's a mini-crisis that they just found out about five minutes before the date, only they can't do anything about it just then. It weighs on their mind, and they don't really have the luxury of focusing on you right now. It's possible that you could be sitting across from the right person on the wrong day.

- *A glaring deal-breaker* that you find out about right up front. Oops! They're wearing a ring. Or hmm, they seem not to have bathed in a week, and you have olfactory evidence to support this thesis.

- *A lack of personal skills.* If this describes your date, keep an open mind. There are plenty of terrific people who just don't impress anybody when they're on a date. Maybe the lack of personal skills will eventually present other problems, but maybe not. Proceed with caution, but don't be too quick to dismiss someone.

C'est l'amour. If you keep bad dates in perspective, they don't hurt as much. Assume that they'll happen, and assume that they're just part of the tax you pay on finding true love. Carry on and enjoy the good ones when they come along.

WHEN GOOD DATES HAPPEN TO GOOD PEOPLE, BUT NOTHING GOOD RESULTS

One of the more discouraging aspects of dating is the situation in which you go out with somebody who seems really right for you, and you have a great time together! And then...nothing. Nada. No follow up date, maybe not even a phone call. Just mystery and frustration. This happened to me, it's happened to friends, it's happened to clients, and it might have happened to you.

Ways that seemingly good dates can go awry:

- *Someone waiting in the wings.* Maybe they just had a great third date with someone else and are about to have a conversation in which they hope to agree to see that other person exclusively, but they aren't sure and are keeping their date with you to be polite and to stay open to the possibility.

- *A deal-breaker you don't know about,* and they don't tell you about. What you wear, what you say halfway through the date...who knows? Not everyone is sensible about dating. They might genuinely like you, and they might have had a great time with you, but they've made up their mind that however terrific you might be, they're not going to get with you because of the deal-breaker. You might have mentioned in conversation that you love the same thing that their ex loved, and they decide that you must have the same character flaws as their ex. Could be anything.

- *Misreading people.* It seemed like a great date: they were smiling, attentive, laughed at your jokes, and seemed genu-inely interested. That might, of course, mean that they *are* genuinely interested, or it might simply mean that they're good at spending time with others. Some people have great interpersonal skills and will make you feel like a million bucks even if they have no real interest in you. (And vice versa, by the way—sometimes someone who really is interested in you doesn't give you a clue.)

- *Bad timing.* Maybe some personal issue came up for them before or after the date, and things got sidetracked.

- *Unknown.* Love is mysterious.

The point is that you basically don't know where you stand going into a date, and you often don't know where you stand coming out of it.

Don't expect *anything* out of *any* date, beyond a chance to get to know somebody and maybe have a fun or interesting time.

You never know somebody's backstory. You never know what they know.

Just because you have a healthy approach to dating doesn't mean they will. It's entirely possible that they'll be the ones placing too much importance on the date, and that will make them nervous or will make them expect too much of you. (It's very difficult in a single meeting to convince someone that you're the one for them.)

Again, the lesson is that you have to manage your expectations. You have to treat each first meeting as though you're at a cocktail party and making conversation with strangers. You have no expectations in that situation; you just move around, make conversation, and see if you spark a connection with someone.

SEDUCTION SUCKS

If you found this book, you might have found other books on dating. One thing that a lot of those books have in common is a set of techniques for seduction. They tell you how to make yourself irresistible, how to get them chasing you, how to get them in bed. In other words, you have to somehow manipulate them into having a romance with you.

But most of these books don't tell you much about *who* you're seducing. OK, maybe they'll tell you're going to get "gorgeous women" or "any guy," but that doesn't really help.

Think about it. Let's say your seduction techniques work. First you get them to notice you. Then you get them to go on a date. Then before too long you get them into bed, and by this time a relationship is underway. Only—oops!—a few weeks or months in, it turns out they don't have anything in common with you, they don't see the world in the same way, and, well, maybe they're kind of a jerk.

Only now you're in a situation. Hopefully one that hasn't involved anyone moving in with anyone, but you're still entangled. And if there's a spark of some sort—if she's good in bed, if he makes you laugh, if your family likes him, if your friends like her—then you might try a little harder than you should to make this thing work. But you're flogging a dead horse. This isn't the person for you, and never was. You were attracted to them, so you did what you were taught to do with attractive people: you seduced them. Bully for you. You've got skills. Only you're not any closer to finding the right partner, and in fact are in all likelihood a little further from it.

This isn't to say that all seduction is bad, of course. Sometimes it's fun. Sometimes it's reeeeally exciting. If it just so happens to be with the right person, then it's kinda wonderful. Just make sure you know who you're getting involved with, and that you're getting involved for the right reasons.

THE DANGER OF HORMONES

Another thing to consider, in a vein related to the process of social seduction, is the chemical seduction that our bodies subject us to.

It's a cliché that guys will frequently think with their dicks. "Paradise by the Dashboard Light" is a song that achieved great popularity because, apart from the music, many, many people could relate to the lyrics. Guy meets girl, hormones fly, guy badly wants sex with the girl, almost regardless of how unsuitable a partner she might be for him. Girl wants commitment, again regardless of suitability. Somebody is very likely to end up unhappy or frustrated.

It's also well understood that many women in their late 30s will experience a previously dormant desire to have children, even if they'd sworn for years that they didn't want them. Sometimes that might work out beautifully. Other times, a woman will remember too late why it was that she didn't want children in the first place.

When I was single, I had an interesting experience that illustrated perfectly the power of chemical attraction. There was a woman I worked with who took me by surprise. She seemed nice enough, but if we had anything in common other than our employer, I was unaware of it. There was no reason to think she'd have been a good match, even if she were available. But she wasn't. She was married. And she was enough younger than me that she might not have been interested in a bald guy with a greying beard, even if she had been single.

None of that mattered to my hormones. She was almost overwhelmingly attractive to me, to the point that I sometimes blushed in conversation with her, regardless of how mundane the topic. That might not sound so surprising if I were a teenager, but I was north of 40 by this time. I was conscious of how odd it was. I think most observers would have agreed that she was attractive enough, but there were plenty of other attractive women around who had no such effect on me. It was the damnedest thing.

Imagine if she were single and just happened to be attracted to me, too. It would have been so difficult for me to have the mental and emotional discipline to forgo an opportunity to get involved with her, given the overwhelming attraction I felt. I like to think I'd have managed it, but I can't look you in the eye and tell you that I'd have inevitably succeeded.

But that's just what I'm asking you to do. I'm asking you to be aware of what you really want, and when the chemical urge comes upon you to do something you know you'll regret, be ready to say no.

ENJOY THE PROCESS

Focus on the process, not the outcome. Remember, by enjoying the process, you're giving yourself your best chance. You're also executing Plan Be.

Do things that are fun! Dating can/should be exciting. And not necessarily in the ways you think. Sure, sky-diving or bungee jumping can be an amazing experience (if neither of you are terrified of heights), but if you're in the right frame of mind, fun can happen anywhere.

When I was dating, I wrote up an essay for my online profile that described who I was and what I was looking for. I said in my essay that it was all very well and good if we could have a good time down on Cape Cod, but the real challenge was to have a good time on the drive back up through the snarl of Route 3, as we were stuck in traffic. Nancy and I have made exactly that drive more than once, and we always have a good time together.

My friend Ken had a tennis date, and the two of them were enjoying themselves. They sat on the grass talking afterwards, and he said he had to get to a store before it closed. When she expressed disappointment at their time together being over, he thought quickly, and said: "You want to go to Bed...Bath and Beyond?" He made her laugh, and off they went. While they were there she started a pillow fight with him, using the pillows that he was buying. Fun is a great way to start a relationship. If you were designing the perfect date, you might not think to choose Bed, Bath & Beyond, but it worked beautifully for them.

If you make a point of enjoying the process, you might learn new things. You might have a ton of fun doing something you didn't know existed. You might meet cool people. You might meet the person who will lead you to your person. And the whole while you can enjoy the sense of possibility.

TAKE YOUR TIME

It's important to keep in mind that you don't need to rush things. That doesn't mean that when you find your someone you *have* to go slow—when the sparks fly, it's human nature to be excited, and if you're both feeling the same way and feel comfortable with each other, go for it.

It might be that if you're in too much of a rush, you'll scare someone off. They may not be as sure about you as you are about them, and your eagerness might be off-putting.

Another possibility is that you'll make an error in judgment. One client related a story in which she met a guy online and they had a great correspondence, followed by a couple of great phone calls. In her mind, all systems were go. He was bright, funny, attractive, and professed real feelings for her. So she blew right through the red flags—e.g. he only ever communicated with her when he was at work—and was left feeling hurt and confused when suddenly he went absolutely silent. She ultimately got hold of him a couple of weeks later, and he made some unconvincing excuses about being busy, and she never heard from him again. It left her feeling confused and fearful of online dating. If she had simply taken her time and paid attention to her feelings about the red flags, she could have avoided all of that pain and been open and ready when the next one came along.

If you connect with someone, and there's something substantial there, they'll probably stick around. When I spoke with David and Maggie, they were just getting started in their relationship— it had been less than a month since their first kiss. But they'd known each other for longer than that. They worked together as massage therapists, and the attraction was pretty much instantaneous. But Maggie was new to the job and wasn't sure whether an inter-office romance was a good idea. She'd never dated a co-worker before, and she wasn't sure how their manager would react. They figured that since they'd be seeing each other regularly, they'd get ample opportunity to get to know each other, and so they agreed to hold off on the romance.

As they worked together, nothing happened to cool their mutual interest, and over time the inevitable became the actual. Maggie loves his silly, playful side, and she didn't hold against him the fact that he's tall, dark, and handsome. Both of them have been pleased to discover how similarly they think, and how often they seem to be able to read each other's mind. So the relationship seems to be off to a good start.

It was a surprise for David in another way—he'd always been more inclined to act, to do something, to almost construct the relationship. He was pleased to find that this new way worked perfectly well, and that their relationship could just sort of happen.

LET 'EM GROW ON YOU...

How many times have you misjudged someone upon first meeting them? Even if you don't remember when and who, you know you've done this—everybody does. If you're relying solely on the first date to connect with people, you're putting a lot of pressure on those first impressions. Not only your impression of them but also their impression of you. Patience applies here; someone might grow on you. People love to say "I can tell in the first five minutes." Well, good for them. Maybe in some cases they can. But just maybe there are other cases in which they can't tell a thing.

*"You can't depend on your eyes when
your imagination is out of focus"*

—Mark Twain, from
A Connecticut Yankee in King Arthur's Court

When Nell met Robert in school, they traveled in the same social circles, which was too bad from her perspective. She was the quiet, unassuming sort, and while he was interested in her right away, she wasn't so impressed. She found him a bit loud, and his sense of humor kind of obnoxious. Given their circumstances, though, so she couldn't avoid him, even if she didn't share his attraction.

Gradually Nell got to know Robert, and she came to understand that he was smart, and that his sometimes lame jokes were sometimes funny, too. And that he was really a great guy once you got to know him.

You know where this ends—with the two of them becoming inseparable, getting married, raising a family together, and generally having the sort of relationship that you're looking for.

So in hindsight it was actually very fortunate that they traveled in the same circles. If they'd met only on a blind date, chances are negligible that they'd ever have gotten together.

We were out for drinks one night and a woman at the gathering told me about her romantic arc. She had a first date that wasn't much fun, but she decided to keep an open mind, and when he asked again, she accepted. The second date wasn't much better. She didn't dislike him, but there just didn't seem to be much chemistry.

Then came the third date, and she was resolved that she was going to take the opportunity to let him down gently. But a funny thing happened. This time, the conversation was a bit better, and when it was over, they found themselves caught in a rainstorm that extended their time together.

They talked, and they talked some more, and by the time the rain stopped falling, something had taken root. They went on more dates, and she subsequently learned that he too had been unimpressed by dates one and two, and he likewise had planned on letting her down gently.

Here's to the rain that led to a marriage. They were lucky, though—they might have expected too much zing in the first couple of dates, and they could have missed out on each other entirely.

If you're the one who makes the bad impression, it can still work out.

Vanessa was in need of a dog fence. She interviewed a number of contractors, but all of them said that she wasn't offering enough money to do what she wanted to do. She was (in her own words) "the quintessential pissed-off divorcée" at that point, and basically accused them all of taking advantage of her lack of knowledge.

About two weeks later, the most silent of the contractors called her back to say that he had figured out how to do the fence for the money she had. The caveat being that it was a two-person job, which meant that he'd need her help. She would have to take vacation time to do it with him.

Vanessa agreed. He arrived in a downpour on their designated start date. He handed her a shovel and mapped out the post holes. They dug all day in the rain, and over the course of the day, she developed a slightly better grasp of the issues involved in building fences—and a better opinion of that particular contractor. The next day was bright and sunny, and he showed up on time with an electric post hole digger. His actual quote was:

"You aren't just paying for the work. You are paying for the experience to know the best method."

As it happened, the fence never got finished for a variety of reasons, but despite the fact that she started things off on the wrong foot, he grew on her, and she on him. A relationship got started, and they've been married very happily ever since.

These anecdotes are useful examples about the pitfalls of relying too heavily on your first impression. But you're human, and you still have to trust your judgment at an emotional level. Just keep the possibilities in mind, and be aware that a closed mind won't do you any favors.

In the same way that some very bright people are lousy test-takers, some terrific potential partners are lousy at making first impressions, especially under the sometimes suffocating pressure of a first date.

Even if you loathe and are terrified by first dates or dates generally, there is no reason to suppose that it won't be the same or even worse for the person you're going out with.

So if they seem a little drab, if they're not witty and charming, if they don't smile enough or make enough eye contact or talk too much about themselves or talk too little about themselves, cut them a little slack. Think of all the things that can create pressure on a date for you—you just spotted that little hole in your shirt, that burrito you had for lunch is creating gastric problems, you might not have turned off the stove before you left—and realize that those things could be running through the other person's mind, too.

Keep in mind that earlier caveat that some people are terrific at social interactions and will show you a great time. It's hard to be sure about anything on a first date. Someone might seem like a good bet or a bad bet, but the more able you are to keep an open mind, the better your odds of finding love.

...BUT TRUST YOUR GUT

So while we just talked about giving things a chance and letting people grow on you, there comes a point where you just have to trust your gut. If you've got doubts about somebody's character, or if over time you're just not sure you want to be with this person, you should pay attention to those thoughts. Patience is a virtue, but don't get yourself inextricably entwined with somebody who you've had doubts about all along.

I had a long, very difficult first marriage, all because as a 25-year-old, I didn't have enough confidence in my own impressions. I renewed an acquaintance with someone I'd known from college, and she was interesting to me at a time when I was feeling particularly lonely. Though I didn't think of myself in such terms, I was vulnerable.

My gut reaction at the time was that the relationship was a bad idea, but I sympathized with her childhood travails and with her current pain, and I constructed a narrative in my head by which I would show her love, heal her, and live happily ever after with her.

Of course it didn't work. Her pain was too profound for me to fix it for her, and though I was stubbornly (and naively) committed to making the marriage work no matter what, it simply wasn't ever going to happen, no matter how hard I tried.

My gut said no right away, but I didn't trust it. And I paid for that in a big way. You can do better than I did.

AGAIN, THIS IS NOT YOUR SPOUSE

As briefly mentioned earlier, any given person that you connect with is very unlikely to be your spouse. That's an important point to remember, not only for the sake of enjoying your time together, but because, on the off chance that this person could become your spouse, you're perversely making your chances worse by putting that kind of pressure on it.

RECOGNIZE THEM WHEN YOU SEE THEM... AND WHEN YOU DON'T

In keeping with the theme of letting people grow on you and trusting your gut, there comes a point where you have to recognize when somebody is right for you. Just as important, you have to recognize when someone *isn't* right for you.

Rachel was pretty good at the "isn't" part. She was a lister—she had expectations for the kind of guy she wanted, and she was adept at finding the various attributes of different guys that were deal-breakers for her.

She'd been in and ended a five-year relationship with a younger guy who just wasn't ready for any sort of serious commitment, and she began to date online. Match.com, eHarmony, jdate— whatever she could think of. She even got on a very expensive, high-end dating site that gave her a free trial because she made a great candidate for many of the well-heeled men on the site. She met some nice guys, some interesting guys, but no forever-and-ever guys.

So there she was at 38, hoping to find someone and start a family, and fending off guys at every turn. Which is a good practice to follow....as long as you're not fending off the right one.

She met Andre on Yahoo! personals. She had two other possibilities at the time who she'd met online, but she had learned not to take any of them too seriously until she was sure they were going somewhere.

Andre was like a lot of guys: he had his good points, but she had her reservations. She's pretty sociable, and he was pretty quiet, and that felt like an imperfect fit to her. And, well, he had hair on his back, which was a turn-off for her. But he was a nice guy, and he took her to the symphony early on; he seemed to be tuned in to things she might like. Moreover, she was grateful that unlike a lot of guys, he didn't (as she put it) "try to stick his tongue down my throat" in the first couple of dates. He seemed to be taking seriously the possibility of a relationship.

Then she went to a good friend's wedding. Her friend had met her new husband on Match.com, and later that evening, when the wedding was over, the gang went out for drinks. Rachel had a heart-to-heart with the new bride about her own dating situation. She mentioned Andre and expressed her reservations. Her friend, who was actually five years younger than Rachel, said "When are you going to grow up?!"

BOOM! That one hit home with Rachel. Maybe she really did have somewhat immature expectations of a potential partner, and she immediately sensed that her friend might be on to something.

Thus reality-checked, Rachel decided to keep an open mind and see where things might go with Andre.

Where they went was that, contrary to her expectations, the Indiana-born Rachel had a great deal in common with the French-born Andre. Cultures aside, they had similar values and similar tastes, and the more she got to know him, the more appealing he became. She soon got rid of the other dating-site guys. The attraction to Andre got stronger and stronger, and soon she'd forgotten all about the back hair thing. Love is like that sometimes. And his reserved personality started to feel complementary: she was social enough for the two of them.

Lisette had a different recognition problem. She always found men attractive, but as a good girl in a Catholic high school, she'd gotten the message loud and clear that she shouldn't be messing around with the boys, which might lead to all sorts of sins. Nobody said anything about girls, however, and when she was a senior, she experimented sexually with one of her friends over the course of a few months. It was pretty clearly a transgression of some sort, but it was much safer than having sex with a boy, and it seemed like a reasonable alternative. She graduated in due course and left that friend behind.

There's a time and a place for everything, and it's called college. Lisette didn't actually try everything, but she tried some things. She started dating guys, and she and her roommate, who were best friends, would often go on double dates together. Just two straight friends having a good time together. Only their good times together extended beyond the usual definition of straight. They had a fling, and while they insisted on their straightness, they thought of themselves as open-minded and enlightened experimenters who were simply enjoying their close relationship.

While she had these intense sexual connections with her female friends, she still looked at guys as the hot ones. They turned her head; she preferred their bodies. She kept dating them, but somehow never connected on a deeper level with them. This she chalked up to having impossibly high standards.

Mr. Right was proving elusive, so she went online and met a few guys on Match.com. One of them seemed like a keeper: she could check off all of those boxes. Finally, someone met her impossibly high standards!

So Lisette gave it a chance. In the midst of getting it on with her perfect guy, she came to the awkward realization that she just plain didn't enjoy sex with men. Nothing wrong with Mr. Right's technique; she just didn't feel the connection that she'd felt with women. And hadn't with any of the guys she'd been with.

She broke that off and came to the realization that she was gay. She uses this term for herself; "lesbian" to her seems to have a connotation of exclusion of men. To this day, the guys are still the ones that turn her head; it's just that for her, deep connection, good sex, and real love all come from women.

She edited her Match profile to say that she was bi and started looking for women. She was surprised to find how little interest she drew that way; she thinks a lot of lesbians are leery of bisexual women, perhaps due to fear of them leaving for a guy.

She realized that, despite her superficial physical attraction for men, she wasn't looking for one. She was gay.

So she updated her profile again, only this time she called herself gay. She met a few women, but no magic ensued. She actually strung along a couple in the hopes that she'd feel something that she didn't.

Part of the problem was that the pool for lesbian/gay women was noticeably smaller than the pool for straight men. So she decided to broaden her search.

She was just 25 when she started identifying as gay, but she always considered herself an old soul, and found experience attractive. So she decided to broaden her search not only in terms of geography—she bumped it up to women within a 40-mile radius—but also in terms of age. She decided that she'd be happy to meet anyone up through the age of 41.

Almost immediately, up popped the profile of a strikingly beautiful and extremely feminine woman named Kara. So beautiful and so feminine, in fact, that Lisette thought she was too good to be true. She had the thought that Kara was out of her league.

Moreover, Kara defied Lisette's expectations of what other lesbians looked like. She couldn't shake the belief that this person was really bisexual, and was probably an adventurer looking to meet someone for a three-way with her husband. Lisette by this time was looking for something real; she didn't want to be anybody's experiment.

Despite all of this, Lisette couldn't stay away. She made the most minimal effort she could by sending Kara a wink, confident that nothing was going to come of it.

To her surprise, the next morning she found a very nice note from Kara. Improbably, Kara was just as interested as she was. Or maybe not so improbably. Lisette couldn't shake her suspicions.

Kara could shake them, though. She wasn't in any hurry to seduce Lisette, and she took her time. It became apparent that Kara was exactly what she said she was, and she was very interested in Lisette, regardless of what their respective leagues might have been.

Love grew, and—hey!—the sex was just like it was supposed to be. Lisette felt a wonderful connection with Kara, and they became exclusive. Within two years Lisette proposed and was accepted.

It took Lisette some time to shake her upbringing and shake the social constructs that said she was supposed to be straight. It was all the more difficult to shake them because of her superficial attraction to men. But her lack of connection with Mr. Right told her what she *wasn't* looking for, and her deep connection with Kara told her what she *was* looking for.

All of this was fascinating to her, and she recently earned a Ph.D. in human sexuality. Bolstered in no small part by her own personal research.

Better late than never: Lisette's recognitions have led her to happiness. It might have taken her a while to figure it all out, but once she did, it didn't take her long at all to find lasting love. Consider whether someone you're seeing is wrong for you, and consider whether that person right in front of you is the right one for you.

GET SOMETHING GOOD OUT OF THE DUD DATES

When you do go out on a date, even the formal kind, keep your expectations low. Not every date leads to a relationship, and not every relationship lasts. Some of those awful first impressions turn out to be accurate. But if you have the right approach, you can get something good out of even the non-starters.

Some good things I've gotten out of dating:

- *Long-term friendships.* I stay in touch with half a dozen women that I met through dating, and I expect to have lifelong connections with some of them. Their presence makes my life better in many different ways, as friendships will.

- *Some action, and some intimacy.* As discussed earlier, when you haven't had any sex in a long time, it can affect your judgment. If sexual desire is part of your agenda, it's hard to see as clearly as when it's not. When somebody validates your attractiveness, you can gain confidence. When someone is intimate with you, you don't feel quite so alone. So even setting aside the sheer fun of it, a little sex now and again might help you toward the big prize.

- *Practice.* Practice will help you get better at all of this, and it might help you gain insights not only into the process, but into yourself and what you want. See the subsequent chapter on this subject.

- *Good advice.* For me, this sometimes came in the form of actual advice, and sometimes came in the form of criticism. A lot of it was useful no matter how it was presented. One woman I saw for a while was offering me some advice, and she said: "Jim, this is what guys who get laid *do!*"

  That was a bit blunt, and of course I was looking for something more than simply getting laid, but her point was really a larger one: if I wanted to find a partner (and I did), there were things I could consider doing to make myself more attractive to more women. I listened, and I learned.

- *A freelance gig.* One of those friends hooked me up with a well-paying part-time job while I was still getting my coaching business off the ground. It was just what I needed at the time, and it was the sort of thing that any good friend might do.

As these examples suggest, I got quite a bit out of dating. I grew as a person, had some great experiences, and learned more about women. By the time I met Nancy, I was ready. Most important, it all made me a better husband.

> **THOUGHT EXPERIMENT**: Can you imagine something useful or interesting growing out of a date with someone who doesn't float your boat romantically? Can you think of two or three things? Go ahead, spell them out. Would the thought of spending time with someone seem more appealing if you were prepared to get any one of those things out of it?

GET SOMETHING GOOD OUT OF YOUR PAST RELATIONSHIPS

A lot of people are angry or bitter or disappointed from previous relationships. Often with very good reasons. You might leave a relationship with nothing else to show for it except the knowledge of what you don't want (or think you don't want). When I was online dating, I'd see profile after profile in which someone would say something like "Please don't be a sports fan" or "please don't be cheap." It seemed obvious that they were reacting almost reflexively to something that bothered them about their ex.

That can be a mistake. Let's say your ex was a creative type who wasn't very good at the details of life. Maybe they were even actively irresponsible. Don't take that single example and decide that you want to avoid artists or musicians or writers. What you have is just one data point, and that's not enough to judge all creative types. Remember, you were attracted to the first one for a reason, or maybe a few reasons. Don't rule out someone who's like all the good parts of your ex, without all the bad.

Which isn't to say that you can't learn what to avoid. Just make sure that you're focused on the essential problem—in this case irresponsibility—and aren't judging others based on the wrong criteria—in this case creativity.

But there's more to get out of your past relationships than learning what to avoid. You can learn about yourself.

Adela wasn't ready for marriage, so she ended a relationship with a guy who wanted a long-term commitment. But she got something valuable out of being with him. She watched him give up on his plans for medical school to follow his dream of being a professional musician. She watched as it made him happy, and she felt envious. Envy led to action, and Adela went back to music school herself. She is continuing to work on her own dream of being a musician.

Caitlyn had been in one relationship for 12 years, ever since she was a freshman in college. So while she had years of relationship experience, it was with a single guy, and there was still plenty to learn about romance and about herself. She met a very attractive guy whose talent she admired, and it was great—Andrew was smart, they laughed constantly, and the sex was rockin'. She thoroughly enjoyed herself until she found that—oops!—he was sleeping around on her and was lying to her about it. She's a trusting sort by nature, and it was a huge blow for her that she couldn't trust him. For her, the lying was worse than the actual infidelity. We all know in a general way that trust, loyalty, and sincerity are important attributes, but having those things taken from her taught Caitlyn just how important they are to her. More important than some of those traditional things that attracted her to a guy.

So she had to break off the relationship.

Caitlyn learned from it, though, and not just in the negative way you're thinking. She's something of an introvert and is very independent. She actively enjoys solitude and figures she's well wired for being single. On the other hand, this relationship was fun! It was exciting, and for a time it made her life better.

It showed her that although she enjoys life being single, there is potential for her to enjoy it even more with the right guy.

Iris is from Mexico City and had dated a series of Mexican guys. Most of the ones she went out with seemed to be immature and threatened by her success in her career as a sales account manager.

Through her work, she met an Irishman named Neil, who was on a project team with her. She was one of the few English speakers in her group, and she and Neil ended up hanging out with the same people after hours. He appealed to her because of his worldliness and otherness—he was a departure from the guys she'd been with. A mutual attraction soon became obvious, and they started seeing each other.

There was little pressure on the relationship—the plan all along was that he'd only be in Mexico for the duration of the project, and since she'd just landed a dream job, she'd stay there to work on her career. But they were grateful for their time together.

About six months in, she was musing to herself and realized that for the first time in her life, she was in a relationship that felt like it was between two equals. Neil was honest, mature, independent, and didn't place demands on her.

When he eventually moved to Boston, their romance came to an end. What she got out of the relationship was a template: she understood that any future relationship should be as healthy as what she had with Neil. She'd never had the notion that she needed a perfect man, unlike several of her girlfriends who have those lists of deal-breakers we discussed earlier in the book. She just wanted the kind of good man that Neil was.

They stayed in touch, and in the meantime she didn't date anyone new. She had little interest in relationships that weren't going to be solid and healthy, and she didn't happen across the right sort of guy for a while.

In one of those little twists that life takes, Iris ended up going to school in Boston in the MBA program at the International School of Business. By the time she got there, she had lots to do at school, and Neil was busy traveling for work, so they didn't resume their relationship.

Besides, while she was there she met Anand, an Indian in her program who had everything that Neil had and more. Neil was the right *type*, but Anand was the right *guy*. Even though Neil was Catholic like she was and Anand was Hindu, the latter seemed to be more on the same page as she was culturally. He was very open, generous, and family-oriented, and she really appreciated those things.

Even though Neil didn't end up as the love of her life, he holds a special place in her memory. Not just because he was the last guy she dated before meeting Anand, but because he was the guy who showed her what she was really looking for; he was the guy that prepared her for Anand.

Cammie also learned something very valuable from a past relationship.

She met her husband in a very conventional way: she was out with a friend, and as they went outside for a smoke (she did that then), a couple of guys were chatting with them. She immediately had a thing going with one of the guys: flirtation, laughter, lots of sparks...probably the alcohol didn't hurt. On the way back in, he held the door for her, and guided her with his arm. And, recognizing the something that was happening between them, he kept guiding her—toward him. More sparks.

She gave him her number, and he used it a couple of days later, which happened to be Patriots Day, also known as Marathon Monday in the greater Boston area. She was at a marathon party, and during the call she invited him over. He joined her, and the rest has been history. As with previous examples, there was no ambiguity, no game-playing, just an immediate connection leading to a healthy relationship.

In some senses, that was no accident. She was ready.

What's interesting about this is the backstory. Cammie had had a troubled relationship with her own family, and a few years earlier, she experienced her first love. He was a very nice guy, and he was from a great family. She knew this firsthand.

She was driving one day and disaster struck. Her attention had wandered, and her car caught the side of the road. She couldn't recover in time. Before she knew it, her car had rolled three times, and she broke her back in the process. It didn't paralyze her, but she was hospitalized and unconscious, and Gary came to visit her. The nurse told her that while she was unconscious, he held her hand, and her blood pressure immediately dropped significantly.

That's not the half of it, though. It wasn't just Gary that was loving. It was his whole family. They took her in while she recovered, for a whole year. She became part of the family.

Eventually she went off to college, and it became apparent that she and Gary wanted different things out of life. Over time they could feel themselves drifting apart, and eventually the relationship ran its course, and Cammie moved on.

She didn't move on empty handed, however. She'd spent a whole year living with his family, and absorbing the lessons that they had to offer. She saw a happy marriage and saw what real partnership looked like. She saw a healthy relationship between parents and children, in contrast to her own family experience.

So when she had her only-too-easy connection with Gary, she was ready for the relationship. Her adopted family had shown her how to be a spouse, how to be a mother, and how to be a *person*.

Though her relationship with Gary "didn't work" in the sense of a long-term romance, it worked very well in terms of making her life better.

There are many, many ways to profit from a relationship. See what you can get out of yours. Whether or not you find eternal love, you can almost always learn about yourself, and that can help you with the next one.

PRACTICE MAKES PRETTY GOOD

The expression is "Practice makes perfect." That might work well for reciting your alphabet, but dating is way too complicated—*people* are way too complicated—for anyone to be perfect at it. So let's work on being pretty good at it.

Peg got better at dating simply by doing it. She'd always told people that dating wasn't her forte. She started out thinking she had to be something she wasn't. She grew up with self-esteem issues stemming from childhood obesity, and she never thought she looked good enough. So she found herself dressing in ways that she never would normally, because she thought it was what was expected of her.

Like so many of us, she was nervous on dates, to the point where she'd find herself blushing when simply saying hello. Gradually she got comfortable with dating, and in the process she was more accepting of herself. She started dressing for dates the way she dressed for life, and she started acting like herself. By the time she met Jason, he got to meet the real Peg, and he very much liked the real Peg.

You can also get relationship practice. When I was dating, I had a few relationships that didn't turn into anything long-term, but they were still useful to me. I got used to the concept of having a normal, give-and-take relationship, in which we discussed what we wanted from each other, what we could do for each other, how we should exist when we were together.

I learned more about women, both in general and in the specific. I learned a few patterns and got better at picking up certain signals. I got comfortable with the concept of going out with someone and with trying out a relationship, without it seeming like the end of the world if things didn't work out.

PATIENCE

If you're clear about what you want, and clear about the challenges before you, you're in good position to be patient. Patience benefits you in more than one way when you're looking for love.

> *"Patience is more than waiting. Patience is knowing what you're waiting for."*
>
> – Unknown

It keeps you in the game. Plan in advance for the ups and downs, and see them for what they are. You're still going to feel all of your emotions in the short term—this business isn't easy. But perspective goes a long, long way. If and when you find your partner, the amount of time it took will seem almost irrelevant.

I went through a lot of life before I met Nancy, but I'm really glad it all played out the way it did. Maybe I could have found somebody reasonable a long time ago, someone sane and decent, with whom I could have made things work, even if it wasn't great. Maybe I'd have been vaguely dissatisfied for a while and deeply dissatisfied as the years passed. How much better that it took the time and effort that it took, and I ended up with Nancy.

Patience is useful not only for the long haul of looking for a lover but also in giving a relationship a chance to breathe and grow.

Daniel thought he was ready to date, even though his divorce wasn't final. Emotionally, he was ready to move on and ready to give his attention to someone new. But he was overburdened

He and Rhonda got together through online dating. They met and had a long conversation—great start. They met again and had a very nice dinner, but Daniel had a lot on his plate (pun intended) with his divorce coming up. Rhonda, a patient person by nature, sensed this. She told him that she could tell he needed space to finalize the divorce. Daniel felt incredibly relieved, not only because he could use that space but because he so appreciated that someone was seeing what he needed and was happy to give him a break.

They kept it to email for about a month, and after the next time they met, he realized there was no point in talking to anyone else. The fact that Rhonda had been concerned about him gave him confidence that she was the right person to pursue. Had she been in a rush to seal the deal, he might not have been ready, and it might have gone awry. Instead, their relationship started with a solid foundation and quickly strengthened. They bought a house together and are now engaged.

Rhonda and Daniel exhibited patience, but they communicated clearly, and as a result they had the luxury of understanding the level of their mutual interest. Sometimes it's different than that.

Theo was in a band, and Yvette was the girlfriend of another band member, Carl. Theo was becoming smitten with Yvette. She wasn't available to him at that moment, which was became all the harder before long because the whole gang started sharing a house. Eventually the band broke up, and so did Yvette and Carl.

This was Theo's cue, or so he hoped. He confessed to Yvette that he was in love with her. Alas, it was unrequited, and she shot him down in no uncertain terms. They continued being friends, and after some time had passed, Theo spilled his guts again. Same response. In the meantime he at least tried to date other women, but none of them impressed him as she did.

Time continued to wear on. Yvette changed, matured, and reorganized her priorities. Eventually she realized that she was developing feelings for Theo, but after shooting him down twice, she figured she'd blown it. But Theo was clear all along on what he wanted, and one day, he just couldn't help but make one last try. Only this time she didn't shoot him down. This time she told him that she loved him right back. They got together, got married, and are happily raising two children.

In truth, she almost *had* blown it—not because of her previous rejections of Theo but because of her inability to tell him how she felt. Fear of being rejected herself got in the way. But Theo's patience overcame that.

Heather and Arthur waited even longer than that. They met in high school in Tennessee, in the same foreign exchange program that took them to Japan for a couple of weeks. They hit it off and immediately became friends. Eventually they started dating, and they felt a real bond between them. But they were still in high school. Heather knew they were young; she knew college would change things; she knew they should grant each other the freedom to date other people and see what the world had to offer.

So they dated other people, and that was fun and exciting for her. But there was just one thing: all of the guys Heather dated just weren't Arthur. He was her gold standard, and those other hapless guys just couldn't measure up. Also, for all of her mature decision-making, she couldn't help but be horribly jealous about the girls that Arthur was dating. Enough was enough, and during their senior year in college, they decided to get back together.

After college, Arthur went off to grad school in Boston, and he asked Heather to join him there. She decided to go for it, and found a job. They still maintained some distance by living separately until marriage, but now the relationship had the chance to get serious. They plugged into a church community and got great support from family and friends. Among their friends were a few happy couples they admired who had been high school sweethearts, which validated the idea for Heather. A couple of years later they got engaged, got married, and now have three children.

We can only speculate what would have happened had they insisted on staying together the whole way. In their youth, they might have made mistakes that hurt each other or otherwise damaged their relationship. Even if everything had gone well, they might have wondered who else was out there and whether they were really with the right person. By exhibiting some patience, they avoided those potential pitfalls and came to understand in a deep way that they were right for each other.

Richard had no choice but to be patient. For a couple of years, he was the token gay guy in the Hillel organization at the University of Pennsylvania. Then one day Laszlo came out of his closet, and now Richard wasn't the only one. They'd already known each other, but they bonded and became better friends, and there it stood for a while. It wasn't long, however, before a mutual attraction became obvious. They started seeing each other.

Just one problem: Laszlo was getting ready to graduate, but Richard was still a junior. College romances are fragile enough; it's all the tougher when half of the couple leaves and heads out into the world. And Laszlo didn't just head out into Greater Philadelphia—he went to Europe to do some touring. When he came back to the States to start working, he landed in New York City.

All the while Richard and Laszlo communicated, and they worked on their relationship. It survived that first year, and then when Richard graduated, his career path pulled him to Boston. Because Richard is a program manager, scheduling is second nature to him, so he quickly set about organizing his life so that he could spend weekends with Laszlo. Fortunately, his manager was understanding, and allowed him to work remotely one day a week.

After another year, Laszlo moved to Boston, and they've been going strong ever since. By being patient and keeping their eyes on the prize, they were able to weather graduation, overseas travel, and a couple of years in different cities. And they're just as happy now as if they'd never been apart. Or maybe even more so, because they displayed such a solid commitment to each other.

DILIGENCE

Patience also fosters diligence. Diligence means persistent effort over time. It's not about *volume* of effort; it's about *consistency* of effort. If you dive in head first, work your tail off to find someone and go on a bunch of dates that come to nothing (or worse still, get no dates at all), you might burn out, curse dating, curse all men or curse all women, and give up entirely. Giving up is not the best way to find love.

Instead, figure out how to be diligent in a way that will work for you.

For example, some people do well with online dating, but others don't. It's the best way to find a lot of single people, and wealthy, tall, slim, gorgeous, and articulate people get lots of attention this way. If you're none of those things, or maybe if you live in a remote location, it can be difficult. That doesn't mean it might not be worth it to put together a nice profile, but it's entirely possible that spending too much energy on online dating will be counterproductive for you.

Some people who might not come across well online do much better when they have a quiet, one-on-one conversation. If that's you, it might be worth figuring out how best to meet singles in your area in a setting that plays to your strengths.

If you're having fun and being efficient, you'll have more emotional energy to give to your effort, and you'll be more diligent. You'll keep trying at your own pace.

Tatum is a children's librarian, a line of work that does not lend itself to finding single guys. She knew that she'd need to find another way. She decided that online dating was the likeliest way for her to find someone. She resolved that she was going to keep at it until she found love.

It wasn't easy. She met guys but had very few second dates. She felt like the world was full of strangers: she was meeting guys who shared no friends, no interests, and no background with her. They had no shared context at all, so that even after a few dates they still seemed foreign.

Tatum realized that it takes a long time to really know somebody well. It took years, with little to show for it, but she relied upon her resolve.

When at last she met Joel, she wasn't initially enchanted by him. He seemed nice, and they had a reasonably good time, so she figured she might as well see where this was going. Unfortunately, Joel was a little off on the second date and seemed awkward. Tatum was put off, and she considered not going out with him again. But mindful of her experience that it took a while to get to know someone, she decided to give him another try.

Sure enough, the third date was better. Much better. They kept dating, and soon a bona fide romance was underway; they married while I was writing this book. Diligence pays.

> **THOUGHT EXPERIMENT:** How many people would you be willing to try connecting with if the end result were finding the love of your life? When people hear that I went out with 69 women, they think that's a lot, but nobody thinks it was foolish of me to do, because—hey—it worked! Would you do it, if you thought it could work? Would you go out with 69 people? Or would you do without a lifetime of happiness simply because you didn't want to invest the effort?

OUTSIDE THE BOX

There are lots of ways to meet people, and it's always good when you can do it while you're doing things that make you happy. Sometimes, however, your favorite activities don't put you in contact with the sorts of interesting people you might want to pair up with. In these cases it pays to think outside the box. Be creative, and when an opportunity arises, take it.

Tina was living and working in DC, and was single and looking. She often talked about it with a co-worker, and one day they decided to try speed dating. Whatever works, right? Well, it didn't.

It was an interesting enough experience, but the selection of available guys just wasn't what they'd hoped, and neither of them ran across anyone who generated any sparks.

They were hanging out at the bar where it had taken place, and the owner of the speed dating company approached them. He said he'd just bought the business and was trying to develop it. He offered to buy Tina and her friend dinner if they'd let him pick their brains for suggestions on how to make it better. Sounded good to them.

They had a long talk, and by the end of the night, he asked them if they'd be willing to help him again. He'd buy them drinks if they'd pass out coupons. They put their heads together and reasoned that this would be a good way to meet guys.

Normally they did the usual passive thing that women are social-ized to do in our society: they'd try to make themselves attractive and available and hope that someone good would stop by and talk with them. But sometimes the guys never came over. Now they had a golden excuse to make the first move themselves, and they even got to pick out the guys.

So on a Friday night in Bethesda, they went out to Rock Bottom and started passing out coupons. At one point Tina attempted to give a coupon to a guy who she hadn't realized was married. She quickly apologized and turned to the guy next to him, named Carter. They struck up a pleasant conversation, and it developed that Carter was an engineer. It just so happened that she was a recruiter, and engineers were among the job descriptions that she was recruiting for.

Great minds think alike: they both quickly realized that they had a professional excuse to stay in contact, in case he needed a job and she needed an engineer. They eagerly exchanged information, and a correspondence was underway, even if their interest wasn't entirely professional. Their correspondence led to a romance that led to a marriage.

The more obvious approach of speed-dating hadn't worked, but Tina didn't let that deter her. She immediately seized upon another opportunity to meet guys, and it paid off when she met Carter. Once that door was open, she seized another opportunity to stay in touch with him.

Sometimes the unconventional approach is completely unplanned. Ariel, a writer, was single and in transitional mode, which she described as the end of a wild ride. She'd recently been through a divorce and since then had been on a bunch of dates, some with nice guys, some with players...she was meeting all kinds.

She was feeling like she needed a change. Maybe she should even move. She was in Hanover, New Hampshire and writing at a favored spot called Rosey Jeke's Café. She was facing the door, which positioned her well to look around, to eavesdrop, to daydream—all part of her writing process.

While daydreaming, Ariel began to think—perhaps a bit wistfully--of an old friend named John. He was nice, he was cute... but the timing had been way off. She wasn't even sure why she was thinking of him now; maybe she just needed to feel happy and connected. But then something remarkable happened—he walked in the door!

She immediately jumped up, ran to him, threw her arms around him, and planted a big kiss on his cheek.

Just one thing: in the split second before her lips landed, she came to the uncomfortable realization that—oops!—this was not John after all, but a complete stranger! By then it was too late to stop her momentum. He looked startled, and she turned a deep shade of crimson as she fumbled with her apologetic explanation.

It's safe to say that, mistake or not, her actions served as an icebreaker. The actual guy, whose name is Stephen, recovered enough to ask "Now that we've embraced, shall we have coffee?"

This was actually completely out of character for Ariel. She describes herself as uptight and not spontaneous at all. And she says Michael isn't spontaneous either. But she was sort of exhilarated in the moment, realizing that she'd done something crazy, something that might change everything. And it did. Regardless of their usual modus operandi, it seemed they were both ready to find each other.

It developed that they knew a ton of people in common, but somehow it hadn't occurred to any of their mutual friends to introduce them to each other. They could easily have met earlier, and in a much more conventional way. That didn't happen. Instead they took advantage of her rather spectacular faux pas, and by the end of their third date, she knew she'd spend the rest of her life with him.

ACCIDENTS HAPPEN

Accidents happen, and sometimes that's a good thing.

Michelle tells the story of an ill-fated romance that her sister Jennifer once had, with a guy we'll call Sam. She dated Sam for a while, but all the while, the two sisters couldn't shake the feeling that this guy was something of a player. After a while, the guy broke it off, with no reason given.

Fast forward a year and a half. One evening Michelle and Jennifer were out on the town and bumped into Sam. By now Jennifer was well over him. Michelle got a call from him a short time later, saying that he had a friend Stu who had seen Michelle at their recent meeting, and thought she was beautiful. He really wanted to meet her. Maybe the two guys could go on a double date with Michelle and Jennifer? Michelle, flattered and single, was willing to give it a try. Jennifer was less enthusiastic, but she was willing to go along in order to support her sister.

Michelle really liked Stu, and things seemed to click between them. So far, so good. She waited for the follow-up call from her new suitor. And waited. Huh? Hadn't they clicked? Hadn't he been into her?

Michelle decided to take matters into her own hands (a great idea!) and called Stu. He was happy to go out with her again, and a romance soon got rolling, resulting in their marriage.

One day the two of them were talking and reviewing how they got together. The funny thing was, their stories differed. In Stu's retelling, Sam had let him know that Michelle was smitten with *him* at that first meeting and wondered if *he'd* be up for a double date?

It appeared that Sam, ever the player, had been having second thoughts about Jennifer, and had fabricated the tales of admiration as an excuse to get back together with Jennifer. But still no luck for Sam—he'd blown his opportunity a year and a half earlier.

It probably never occurred to him—or occurred to him to even care—that the happy ending would come not for him, but for Michelle and Stu, who are still enjoying the benefits of their completely accidental relationship.

TELL THE WORLD

Let people you know that you'd like to find somebody special.

If your friends and co-workers know you want to meet someone, they're more likely to think of you when they're talking to that person who could be perfect for you. Or they might start to look at you a different way themselves.

It's not unusual in contemporary society for us to isolate ourselves to some extent. When it comes to affairs of the heart, this can be magnified. There might not be many or even any who you feel entirely comfortable discussing your love life with. That can be an obstacle, but you can and probably should try to overcome it.

If you're feeling sheepish or embarrassed, consider what you actually have to lose, and what you have to gain. Let's review:

THINGS TO GAIN	THINGS TO LOSE
An introduction to someone single and interesting whom you might never have met if you hadn't mentioned you were looking.	A bit of time lost meeting someone single and uninteresting whom you might never have met if you hadn't mentioned you were looking.

Suggestions from a friend about how to meet someone great.	Missing out on that story your friend was going to tell you about how their car wouldn't start that morning.
Your secret admirer working up the courage to flirt with you or just to talk to you, leading either to romance or the simple knowledge that somebody admires you.	Having to gently imply to the wrong secret admirer that you don't secretly admire them back.
Friends keeping an eye out for interesting candidates for you.	Being mildly embarrassed because your friends knowing that you're looking for love....*just like pretty much every other single person on the planet.*
Love.	Absence of love.

What you have to lose is not much—whatever your vague fear is about what they'll think, it really won't affect your life much—and what you have to gain is substantial: you can get inspiration from friends, ideas, advice, and moral support. And they can identify potential partners for you, as amateur matchmakers. Matchmaking is an old and honored profession, and you can either let your friends do their best, or you can improve your chances by hiring someone like my friend Carol Steinfeld, who does it professionally and knows what she's doing.

Jeff and Joanie had in one sense known each other all their lives: they grew up in the same class in the same Massachusetts schools. But they were never close, and even though they ended up in the same town in adulthood, somehow they never crossed paths.

Lori, Joanie's neighbor and a good friend of Jeff's sister, was on the job. Lori knew that Jeff was single and that Joanie was single, and she thought they'd make a great couple, so she worked on getting them together. She kept dropping hints to Joanie, and Jeff likewise heard from his sister. Neither thought too much about it, but the groundwork was being done.

So when one fine day they happened to bump into each other in the lobby of a Boston building, they were prepared, and they recognized each other. They'd been hearing lots of good things about each other, so they struck up a friendly conversation, and decided to keep in touch. He called soon after, and two life-long singles got married—a first for each—at the age of 49.

Of course, not all set-ups result in relationships. And other set-ups might require a little time to work...

Tarae and Brandyn met as freshman at Cornell. They were both part of the modestly sized black community there, and a mutual friend tried to set them up. Neither one of them was ready for that, because they both had plans. They were both public school kids who wanted to figure out the lay of the land in a demanding Ivy League environment so they could succeed both academically and socially. They had more important things to focus on than romance.

This shared mindset did draw them together as friends. They admired each other, and supported each other, and were both quite happy with this arrangement, regardless of what the mutual friend thought. But there was plenty to like romantically, and their respect-based friendship grew until eventually they crossed over to a romantic relationship.

Even then, they were in no rush. Both had plans, and those plans involved law school and graduate school and law practice and geography and a great deal of communication and planning. A full decade after they were first met, they finally got married. But the seed had been planted years before by a friend who knew they were both single and available.

STRATEGIZE

So what's going to work best for you? You know your usual things to try. Some have worked, some haven't (at least not yet). Can you give something else a shot?

A small list of different things to try:

- An online dating site

- A dating app (really just another kind of online dating)

- A professional matchmaker

- Asking a friend or relative if they know someone to match you up with

- An online meetup group for something new that interests you (see e.g. meetup.com)

- Striking up a conversation at the supermarket

- Jumping into a Facebook conversation with a friend of a friend

- Hanging out at a coffee shop

- Offering an opinion at a museum

Anything is good as long as it's feels like something that's worth doing *for you*. The important thing is to get out there, whether physically or online, and meet people.

Err on the side of going out. Err on the side of making connections. Here are some words and phrases for you to consider using when somebody suggests doing something:

- "Yes!"

- "OK."

- "Where and when?"

- "You betcha!"

- "Why not?"

- "Sure!"

- "Hell yeah!"

You can retain the right to pass if you have a schedule conflict, if you're exhausted, or if you just dread whatever the situation is. But keep the principle in mind: whenever you think you might be up to getting out and meeting someone, go for it. And keep the larger principle in mind: strategize, and give yourself your best chance.

RELAX

We've talked a bit about this, but it's important enough that it bears repeating:

Relax.

Easier said than done, huh? For so many people, the nerves take over when they find themselves confronted with someone they're attracted to. It's part insecurity—"She's so great! How could she possibly be interested in me?"—and part over-investment—"I've been looking for so long, and here he is! I can't mess this up!"

Seriously, relax. Love is hard. This one probably isn't "the" one, even if they sure seem appealing. You might learn subsequently that they aren't as good a deal as you thought, or it might be that there's some reason that they're just not going to be interested in you no matter how terrific you are. You just can't assume anything about any given person. And if you can't assume anything, then there's no reason to get heavily invested in the outcome of a given date.

I've always had lots of female friends and never had a problem talking to girls when I was young…unless of course she was the one I had a life-threatening crush on. Then I was a tongue-tied mess.

It's not just young people that this happens to, either. I had a client in his late 30s who had lots going for him—tall, athletic, handsome, well-employed. He always seemed to have at least three women who were interested in him at any given time. And the same conditions applied: if he wasn't particularly interested in them, he relaxed, and they all thought he was great. And several of them wanted more from him than he was prepared to give.

Any woman he really liked, on the other hand, made him nervous. He was afraid of screwing things up, and it became a self-fulfilling prophesy: he'd be too eager, and she'd think he was too intense, and back off from him. It happened over and over again.

Same guy, different results. Relax and be yourself, and when you do stumble across the person who could end up being your partner, you'll be at your best.

CHECK OUT YOUR FRIENDS

Check out your friends as you're looking for your lover. Lots and lots and lots of people report having romantic feelings for a friend, but they don't act on those feelings, perhaps because they're afraid they'll screw up the friendship.

Now, maybe this is based on a subconscious understanding that their friend isn't really their life's partner. It's entirely possible to genuinely love someone you can't successfully connect to romantically, and that's OK. Maybe you just never felt it, or maybe you see the world differently and don't quite fit together as a couple. If that's the situation you're in, cool. That's what friends are for—carry on.

But other times, the two of you are just sort of dancing around each other, happy enough in the friendship—and maybe fearing rejection. You know what to do in that situation. Find out. Probe. If you think it's there, you can even discuss it directly, maybe as a hypothetical. "Can you imagine us as a couple?" Then probe again.

The third situation, the one that worries everyone, is that romantic feelings are unrequited. That one sucks, but—what's the phrase?—tough shit. Finding the right partner trumps all. If your friendship is really solid, it can probably survive unrequited love, so long as you're respectful of your friend's decision. Usually, they will at the very least be a little flattered by your interest and will feel warmly toward you, as long as you honor the friendship.

In some cases it might go awry, and you'll lose a friend. That will hurt. But I go back to the words of my cousin Monica. One day we were talking, and I was lamenting my loneliness. She encouraged me to take comfort in my friendships. I pointed out that friends come and friends go, and she told me: "Listen to what you just said." Her point was that while some friendships do fade away, they are often replaced by new friendships that might be just as rewarding or even more so. She wasn't letting me get away with feeling sorry for myself.

In the case of a particularly close friend, it might be hard to replace them, and that might be painful. But even good friends might drift apart: you might move, your friends might get married or have kids, or someone has a parent who gets sick, and while you're still friends, you just don't see as much of each other as you used to. While you should treasure your friendships , recognize that the circumstances of a friendship can change over time.

So if you're fearing what will happen to your friendship if you make romantic overtures, don't. It's a gamble you're going to have to take, if you think they might be the one.

Atara met Doug their freshman year of college, before classes had even begun. They hit it off right away as friends, but that was all. Atara is an introvert, and she believed that her happiness didn't depend on someone else. She knew instinctively that it was better to be alone than to be with the wrong person.

A couple of years went by. There were times when she or Doug felt some romantic interest, but circumstances were never quite right: when one person started to think that way, it seemed the other was dating someone.

One day, Atara came over to visit Doug's housemate, who was not there. She and Doug went for a walk instead. That mutual romantic interest was now front and center. As they walked, they gradually warmed up to discussing what they were really feeling for each other.

They realized that they had to get together. Doug was still in a long-distance relationship at the time, but he knew that his current girlfriend wasn't the one for him. Atara was, so he made the difficult phone call.

No fuss, no drama, no lightning bolt. Just a deep friendship that developed into something more. The physical part happened slowly, but it happened. Eventually their lives turned in such a way that they had to have a long-distance relationship of their own. This was before cell phones and Facebook and relatively easy communication, so their relationship depended on the depth of their friendship. Which turned out to be enough, and they've been together—and still the best of friends—ever since.

> **THOUGHT EXPERIMENT:** Have you ever been attracted to a friend, but you couldn't quite bring yourself to express that to them? What would have happened if you had let them know? Apart from a potential awkward moment or two, would it have made your life significantly worse if you'd asked and they said "No, thanks"? Might it have made your life better if they said "Great!"? Maybe you could even write a letter without sending it, and try writing responses to it, both positive and negative. If you can imagine both outcomes, it might be easier to take the plunge and ask the question.

PAY ATTENTION TO YOUR CO-WORKERS

Sandra interviewed for a new job, and got it. Her interviewer, Jerry, was single, blond, and blue-eyed.

Some of her co-workers had the notion that Sandra and Jerry would make a good couple. Nah, Sandra said—he's more the friend type. She had one of those foolish sets of expectations for her partner: she wanted the stereotypical tall, dark type that didn't quite describe Jerry. She'd started off seeing him in professional terms and simply didn't see him as romance material.

They got to know each other as they continued to work together, and she very much enjoyed their relationship. Then it happened that they were both invited to the wedding of another co-worker. It was a romantic setting, and at the reception, alcohol was served. It was a rich enough mixture that Jerry, who'd had his eye on Sandra all along, was emboldened to make his move. And it was a rich enough mixture that Sandra set aside her reservations, and his move succeeded. They found themselves hooking up that night.

In the light of the next morning, Sandra was concerned, and they talked. She wanted to be just friends, and she was afraid that a physical relationship would ruin the friendship. But Jerry said he wanted more than friendship and wanted more than simply a physical relationship. He was smitten from the start, and he even remembered what Sandra had worn to the interview way back when.

Having come this far, he wasn't going to give up easily. He worked on her, and as she was confronted with the issue, she realized that she already understood deep down that he'd make a great husband and father. She started seeing him, and it took. Eventually they married, and her deep-down understanding proved to be correct.

Katya was looking for somebody and was dating online. She was conscious at the time of how superficial the profiles could be and how they present a somewhat artificial image of a prospective date, in much the same way that a resumé might present a somewhat artificial image to a prospective employer.

Then there was Serge, the new guy at work. Katya trains people to do data collection for clinical trials. She was working on a project, and she knew that Serge had expertise that the team could use, so she called him in to help the team.

She was immediately impressed by his intelligence, his focus, and his commitment to helping the team succeed. Instead of having some guy on a date tell her about himself and how great his character was, she got to see it in action with Serge.

As the project continued, they needed to maintain a collaboration, and instant messaging was a favorite way of communicating in her workplace. There was a lot of veiled flirting between the two of them, but she didn't make too much of it: a lot of that goes on among colleagues, whether or not it's serious, and IM lends itself to that sort of thing, in the safety of separation and ambiguity.

Their friendship was developing. She went away on vacation to Hawaii, and when she got back she shared with him that it was the best vacation she'd ever had. One day after work, she showed him the photographs from the trip, and they spent a solid hour together, looking at her pictures. While they were talking, he told her that he was working on a book, and she shared even more with him: she told him that she was working on a short story. Katya is something of an introvert, and this was not something that she'd revealed to many people. They were bonding.

Then came a big presentation that Katya had to deliver to the sales team. She confessed to Serge that she was very nervous about it, and he offered an indirect way of helping: he offered to take her out for drinks after the presentation and said that she could look forward to a friendly face afterward, as a means of helping her cope with the stress. Maybe it was the romantic opportunism, maybe it was his clear desire to be there for her, or maybe it was just the way he said it, but at this point Katya knew that there was something here; this wasn't simply casual flirtation.

They started dating for real, their relationship grew, and they've married. Katya recently gave birth to a little girl.

Some people draw strict lines between work and romance. Of course there are good reasons for proceeding with caution, but the romance that took root between Katya and Serge happened because they were able to develop a rapport with each other and get a sense of each other's character in a professional environment that removed romantic pressure and enabled an authentic connection to form.

DON'T LET OTHERS DECIDE FOR YOU

It's generally a good idea to listen to your friends. They might have valid concerns about a prospective match for you, and those concerns might be worth considering. They might think someone else would be perfect for you, and they might be on to something.

But friends aren't always right, and listening to them is different than doing what they say. They might have all the best intentions, but when push comes to shove, you have to decide who is or isn't right for you.

When Lisa was 21 and fresh out of college, she started a new job. She didn't know a single person there, so when in the first week a softball game was being organized, she signed up so that she could get to know her co-workers.

Lisa was mostly worried about her new career and wasn't actively in the market for a guy, but hey, this one guy was tall, athletic, and handsome, and Lisa couldn't help but notice him. The next day she asked a co-worker about him.

The co-worker promptly warned Lisa off. "That's Bob. Don't waste your time—he won't give you the time of day. He's more into himself."

OK, fair enough. As noted, Lisa wasn't really in the market anyway, so she filed away that information.

A few years went by, and she and Bob had gradually gotten to know each other and become friends. Friendship became attraction became sexual tension. One day they just looked at each other, and realized that they were on the same page. Just like that, a romance was underway that ultimately led to marriage.

Fortunately Lisa had the time and opportunity to get to know Bob, so she could overcome the message she got from her co-worker, which in hindsight could probably be reinterpreted as: "He didn't give *me* the time of day. He's not that into *me*."

The thoughts and suggestions of your friends can be valuable, and you're smart to consider them. But keep in mind that opinions are not the same thing as facts, and that someone else's impressions aren't always completely accurate.

Listen to what they have to say, but keep an open mind, and at all times be honest with yourself.

HOLY $#!&! IT'S YOUR WIFE!

So we just got done saying that you shouldn't let other people decide for you. We also have been saying throughout that you shouldn't invest too much hope or expectation in any one person. Of course, there are exceptions to every rule—sometimes your friend will set you up with just the right person, and sometimes you won't be able to help getting your hopes up. That's all fine, as long as you keep enough perspective that you won't be crushed if things don't work.

Ken met Jess. But he wouldn't have if it weren't for his best friend, Adele. They'd run across a website in which a woman could write up and post a profile of a guy friend for other women to read, and she'd arrange the introductions if there was sufficient interest on both sides. So the guys had been pre-vetted and presented in a way that would presumably be interesting to other women. Adele had been a great friend of Ken's since forever, and she posted a profile for him in hopes that this great guy could find a worthy partner.

In the meantime, Jess was doing the same thing for one or her co-workers. Along the way, she was offered a free trial herself, and she noticed Ken's profile. She shot Adele an email, and a correspondence was underway. Adele forwarded it to Ken, with the subject line "Holy $#!&! It's your wife!"

Good call, Adele. She knew Ken very well and was utterly convinced that he and Jess would be perfect together. She did her thing as matchmaker, and Ken and Jess soon met. They hit it off right away, and they ended up both as life partners and as business partners. That website got acquired and shut down for whatever reason, but flushed with their own success, they've created the website *jessmeetsken.com*. (Where you can get more of the story, by the way.) Updated technology, but the same concept: women put up profiles of their guy friends, and other women can read them, without concern about misrepresentation or questionable intentions.

So there is real opportunity in good old-fashioned matchmaking, whether through a professional, through a good friend, or through a website. As long as you keep your expectations at an appropriate level, any approach that feels comfortable is worth pursuing.

ONE DATE LEADS TO ANOTHER

Sometimes a date with the wrong person can be a catalyst for a date with the right person. Mark was set up with a very nice woman by a mutual friend. Dinner was good, the conversation was pleasant...but no. No chemistry, no mind-meld. Fortunately, his date seemed to have better judgment than his other friend. She set Mark up with a woman she knew who she thought might be just the thing for him. Enter Jeanne. Voilà! Chemistry, mind-meld, romance, marriage, children.

In a similar vein, Aidan's parents were both set up on blind dates. They're Irish Catholic, and they were set up simultaneously with a Jewish man and a Jewish woman, respectively. Those two both had family pressures to find a nice Jewish partner. Which didn't sound all bad to them. So while both thought that their Irish Catholic dates were fine people, they didn't think it would work out for them.

 As luck would have it, the man and the woman were part of the same Jewish community, and they were friends. As they related the stories of their blind dates to each other, the thought occurred to them that their two perfectly nice Irish Catholic dates might be interested in each other. So they set the two of them up.

And it took, resulting in a union that was blessed by Aidan. Not a bad story, but it doesn't quite end there. Just to bring the whole thing full circle, their Irish Catholic son ended up going out with a Jewish girl himself, only in this generation it took: he and Naomi got married.

THE ONE WHO GOT AWAY

Has anyone ever gotten away from you? Someone you were romantically involved with, but for one reason or another it didn't quite work out, or life pulled you apart in some way? If you miss them and find yourself wondering whether that could have worked if only things had been a bit different, consider the fact that maybe things are now a bit different.

People change, circumstances change. If there was a real connection in that relationship, and if your long-ago ex happens to be single, then it might be worth reconsidering whether it might work if you tried it again.

Alexandra and Jay were both students at Georgetown, and they flirted whenever he came into the coffee shop where she worked. It wasn't long before he realized he was on to something good, and he asked her out.

They dated throughout college, and enjoyed each other. He always treated her well; it was a healthy relationship. But then came graduation, and their lives were at a crossroads. Jay was ready to settle down in his beloved Boston, start on his career, and generally get on with being a grown-up. Alexandra was in a different place. She was eager to see the world, and she accepted a position teaching third grade at an American school in Costa Rica. They parted amicably and headed off in different directions.

Alexandra had a few relationships along the way, and life went on. Eventually she decided to go to graduate school and was accepted at Tufts, just outside Boston. She spent the summer before she started there on Nantucket, waiting tables, and soon met and began seeing a carpenter.

One day, she was driving the carpenter's truck on the island, and from out of nowhere, a bike darted in front of her. She slammed on the brakes, swerved, and somehow managed to avoid hitting the cyclist. But as he took his own evasive action, he lost control and went to the ground.

Alexandra rushed out of the truck to make sure that he was OK, not knowing what to expect. It turned out he was OK. It turned out that he was also Jay! Whatever she was expecting, it definitely wasn't *that*. They were amazed to run into each other, both literally and figuratively.

Acquaintance renewed. They exchanged contact information, and he showed up with friends that night at the restaurant where she worked. They both had lots of mutual friends in the young transient culture that blossoms in places like Nantucket every summer, and they started socializing together in groups.

As this was going on, Alexandra was realizing that her carpenter wasn't the guy for her. As she tried on the various relationships she had after Jay, she was conscious of finding someone who would treat her the way he had. The carpenter just wasn't kind enough.

In the meantime, she was seeing a lot of the guy she had let go. His brother watched the two of them, and he couldn't imagine why the two of them didn't get back together. They danced around each other for a while, and the right thing to do became obvious. Alexandra asked a guy out for the first time in her life. She asked Jay.

She got back the one who got away, and they've built a life and a family together.

Alexandra and Jay obviously were really lucky to have crossed paths again in the way they did. There's no reason you need to leave it to chance. If you've already had the kind of connection you're looking for, and you have the opportunity, you might reestablish the lines of communication to see if that long-ago sense of connection still applies.

PUT YOURSELF IN POSITION TO GET LUCKY

Contrast the last story with this one. Timothy is gay, and he was single and looking. Luck threw Joe in his path: Timothy pulled into a park, and there was Joe, getting ready for a bike ride. Timothy was immediately attracted, but he had no idea whether or not Joe was gay.

He decided to stay where he was, read his newspaper, and wait this guy out. And in a way, it worked: Joe said hello and they chatted for a bit. But then he went off on his bike ride, and Timothy was in a quandary. He still had no idea whether Joe was gay, or whether this guy was even attracted to him. But he seemed friendly enough, and it seemed just possible that there might be something there, and by this time Timothy was definitely interested.

The problem was that he had no idea who Joe was, or where he lived, or whether he'd ever see him again. So he employed a time-honored device: he went back to the scene of the meeting the next week, hoping Joe would turn up once again. And damned if it didn't work: there was Joe, and Joe was happy to see him. They were able to strike up a friendship and work their way up to confessing a mutual attraction. They've been together ever since.

Once again, luck was involved, but it's a simple, effective illustration of the point that you should put yourself in position to get lucky. It doesn't matter if the odds aren't great—nothing ventured, nothing gained.

GET YOUR BUTT OUT THE DOOR

You're not likely to meet your special someone by sitting alone in your living room. You've got to get out there, consistently. The more you get out into the world, the more people you'll meet. The more people you meet, the more interesting people you'll meet. The more interesting people you meet, the better your chances of finding the one. Just the way Timothy met Joe in the previous chapter.

Madeline didn't want to go out. It was the middle of the week, and she wasn't really up for it. But her friend wanted to, and Madeline had a car. She was needed. So her friend pressed the issue, and Madeline reluctantly agreed to drive them both to a showing of "The L Word."

Somewhere else in town a very similar conversation was going on. Ana is something of an introvert; she didn't much enjoy going out, and really didn't want to on this particular night. But, as with Madeline, her friend prevailed upon her, and she went.

Fast forward to the show. Upon arriving, Madeline remarked to her friend that the girl over there in the scarf was kind of cute. Just a passing comment, because she really wanted to watch the movie and get out of there. So they watched the show, but nature called, and Madeline went to the restroom. When she got back, her gregarious friend was having an animated conversation with two women, one of whom was the girl in the scarf.

The other two were dominating the conversation, which left Madeline and Ana, the girl in the scarf, to talk to each other. As they talked, they discovered things they had in common. Frida Kahlo? Yes! I love her paintings! Pablo Neruda? Yes! By the time they were done talking, they'd hit it off in a big way, and neither regretted her decision to go out. They exchanged contact information, and a couple of emails and a couple of nights later, they were out dancing together.

They've been together ever since, and now have a little boy. If they'd followed their usual patterns, they'd never have met. Good thing that the peer pressure worked.

Give yourself chances. You don't have to think in terms of something happening on any given outing, but if you get out there often enough, something good can happen.

BE READY FOR SERENDIPITY

The previous chapter was about creating your own luck. But sometimes life intervenes and throws you some luck even though you haven't done a thing to improve your chances. Be ready for one of these breaks, and take advantage if it should arise.

In high school, Amy had the problem that some pretty girls do. Guys were afraid to ask her out, assuming they'd be rejected. (One guy that she had a crush on told her that very thing some years later.) Since she didn't have the flirting skills to bridge the gap, she didn't get asked out by a single boy from her high school.

Partly as a result of that, she married the first guy that showed any serious interest in her. It didn't work.

Some years later, she was waiting tables in Tulsa to pay the bills while trying to get her creative career going. A regular customer named Matt would sometimes chat with her, when he wasn't busy with the dates he'd sometimes bring in. One evening they had a long talk, and as it ended, he said that it had been nice chatting with her. Amy had been holding a coffee pot the whole time, and her arm was killing her, so she said "Yeah, but it would have been nicer if I weren't holding this coffee pot."

She was simply referring to the pain in her arm but, fortunately for both of them, he misinterpreted it to mean that she wished they could talk somewhere else. Thus encouraged, he asked her out, and they clicked in a big way. They've been married for years in what she describes as "a phenomenal relationship."

If Amy hadn't offered that off-handed line, or if it hadn't been misinterpreted, they might never have gotten together. But by having that conversation, they unwittingly each put themselves in a position for something great to happen.

Another bit of serendipity involved my friend Kate. She was young and in full boy-chasing mode. That wasn't what was on her mind when she went to Quaker meeting, though; she was there for spiritual reasons. Just living her life. At the meeting, she found herself right next to the most gorgeous guy she'd ever seen, and, well, so much for spirituality. She couldn't help herself, and she peeked over at him constantly. But he never seemed to look her way, even once. It actually occurred to her in her young hubris that he might be gay. Because really, why else wouldn't he be checking her out?

When Meeting ended, there was a gathering for lunch. Kate stuck around in the specific hope of meeting the guy. Several hours later, neither of them had been able to see their way clear to saying hello. Finally Kate gave up. She stood up and announced to the group that she had bread rising on the counter and had to go home.

As she drove away, she noticed the guy on his bike. She waved to him, and figured that was it. She hadn't been to Meeting in over a year as it was, and didn't know when or if she'd ever see him again.

Then, at a traffic light a few blocks away in Harvard Square, there came a tapping at her window. She rolled it down, and the young man, who'd caught up to her in the heavy traffic, asked her "How important is that bread?" She said "Not at all!"

She joined him——his name was Oliver--at a concert he was going to. They had a great time, and their romance was off and running. He was the first guy she dated who didn't try to change her, and she married him. They have a wonderful relationship that gives her the freedom to act on her dreams and live the meaningful life she'd always wanted.

It was fortunate that they ever got together—she had assumed at the meeting that he wasn't interested in her. He was shy and thought she was beautiful, and he couldn't muster the courage to look over in her direction. They might have missed out on each other entirely if their routes and Cambridge traffic hadn't cooperated to throw them back into each other's paths, and if Oliver hadn't found his courage.

Don't get me wrong—please do not depend on serendipity. You'll have much better chances if you take an active role in your own good fortune. But it sure is nice when everything aligns and you do have a bit of luck—be ready for it, and don't miss your opportunity when it comes along.

DON'T DISQUALIFY YOURSELF

As Kate and Oliver demonstrated, you might miss out on great things by making faulty assumptions. As my friend Tita (one of those former online dates) once told me: "Don't disqualify yourself; let others do that for you."

"But my silent fears have gripped me,
long before I reach the phone,
Long before my tongue has tripped me;
must I always be alone?"

–The Police, "Every Little Thing She Does Is Magic"

In this context, you might be worried that the wonderful, exotic, interesting person in front of you would *never* be interested in a schlub like you. And maybe they aren't interested. But maybe, just maybe, they could *get* interested.

This is an easy point to make, but sometimes it's hard not to disqualify yourself out of the fear of rejection.

Rejection really hurts. Regardless of whether you can convince yourself intellectually that it just wasn't a good fit, or that you were simply misunderstood or underestimated, or that they just happen to be more interested in somebody else at the moment, or any of the myriad other possible explanations for why they might give you a "no, thanks", you don't believe those things emotionally. Emotionally, it feels like you've been dismissed as sub-standard. It's a referendum on who you are. Nobody likes being told that they just aren't wanted.

The good news is that you have the capacity to see the problem coming. Acknowledge that you might be rejected, and that it might happen repeatedly. Decide that you're OK with that, and are going to keep trying regardless. We do this when we're looking for employment; why shouldn't we do it when we're looking for love?

Chalk it up to the cost of finding a great partner. Know that every time you disqualify yourself, there's at least a small chance that you're doing it needlessly. That in disqualifying yourself, you could be missing a golden opportunity to make a wonderful life-long connection.

Kyle had always loved Vermont. His grandparents had a summer place up there, and as a kid his family visited every summer. Moreover, two of his sisters lived there now, and family was important to him. He had moved to New York shortly after college for a gig that was supposed to last five weeks, and he planned on living there no longer than that. But plans go astray, and eight years later, he was still in the big city, a place that never stopped feeling alienating to shy, small-town Kyle. He finally decided to make the big move back to the place he loved.

The catch was that he was single. He wondered what he was doing, leaving a place with a zillion gay men to move to a place with very few. But he decided that what he'd be giving up in quantity, he might be getting back in quality. He couldn't abide the New York bar scene, and maybe Vermont would have more guys he could really connect with.

He was determined to make the best of it, and after he moved, he made up his mind to go to any and every event where other gay people might show up.

He went to with his sister to a one-man play about the experience of being black and gay in Vermont. He saw an attractive man sitting in the front row and remarked to his sister: "See him? He's exactly my type, but that's just the kind that will never pay attention to me."

In other words, Kyle was disqualifying himself. He was basing it on past experience, but of course every experience is unique. The show finished, and as they stood there talking, the man walked by without saying anything. Kyle, feeling validated, said "See?" As if it were front-page news that a stranger happened not to stop and strike up a conversation with another stranger. Or that a gay man might not hit on another man who was talking to a woman.

Kyle was working for an HIV prevention program, and his job required him to go to a big conference. There he was introduced to Jared, one of the volunteers, who just happened to be the man from the front row at the show.

So they met, and they got to know each other, and there was even some flirtation. Jared asked Kyle out twice, but in both cases Kyle had conflicts, and to him it was ambiguous whether he was being asked on a date—maybe the guy just wanted some company.

It might seem like a short step from there to a romance, but the shy Kyle couldn't quite bring himself to bridge that gap. It turns out that Jared had spotted Kyle in church, but Kyle hadn't seen him. Jared knew the congregation, and he knew which people were new, and he'd set his sights on this one. But having found him, he wasn't getting anywhere.

Still, Kyle was pleasant and friendly, so Jared decided to give it one last shot. This time his invitation was accepted, and this time it was definitely a date. Before long, the kind of guy who Kyle thought would never pay attention to him was romancing him, and then marrying him.

But he almost missed out: if they hadn't run into each other again at the right place and time, Kyle's self-disqualification could have cost him dearly.

Then there's Molly's story, with self-disqualification on both sides that likewise nearly sabotaged a great romance.

Molly and Seth knew each other from the time she was three years old. When she was 12, they had their first kiss, and they spent a wonderful summer together before life sent them in different directions for several years. When she was 19 and in community college, they reconnected, and it was great. Molly did well in community college, and transferred to Johns Hopkins. Seth came to visit her there, and she had a fantastic time. So she was floored when he broke it off right after their visit.

She couldn't imagine what she had done wrong, and she couldn't believe he'd dumped her. Things had gone so well! They so obviously clicked!

The break-up sent her into an emotional tailspin. She went as far as removing parts of her phone each night and giving them to different friends, so she wouldn't be able to make a drunken phone call begging Seth to take her back.

What she didn't understand was that Seth, who was a UPS truck driver at the time, had gotten a good look at Johns Hopkins and decided that a regular guy like him would never fit into Molly's big, exciting new world of infinite possibilities. He'd disqualified himself.

Unlike in the previous anecdotes, there were real consequences. Molly met someone else and married him at age 21, right after graduation, thinking that she might as well, since she couldn't have Seth. By age 22, she was pregnant.

The marriage was mostly unhappy: he was an angry man, and she found herself walking on eggshells so as not to set him off. One day, one of their daughters was upsetting him, and he hit her. This enraged Molly, who grabbed a knife and made it very clear to him that he was not going to hit one of their daughters again. She said that instead he should hit *her* first, but she reminded him that he'd have to sleep some time. The message was delivered, but the damage was done, and Molly wasn't any happier.

All this while, she'd seen and envied how her dear friend Deborah was living, in an obviously loving, healthy relationship. Molly had resolved to stick out her own marriage until her daughters got through school, but fortunately for her, Deborah knew better and asked her whether this was the sort of example she wanted to set for her daughters. That logic hit home with Molly, and finally she asked for a divorce.

Then came the day that Seth's mother died. His family and her family had always been close, and her family asked her if she could make the drive from Philadelphia back up to upstate New York, to represent the family at the funeral. She thought she could handle it, so she did it. Of course once there she saw Seth—a knife through the heart. There was the love of her life there with another woman as his wife. She hardly spoke to him and couldn't wait to leave.

His father asked her if she could come back to their house, and she didn't feel that she could refuse, as hard as it was to see Seth. She stuck very close to the father's side the entire time, but she was able to see that something was off with Seth's marriage. And she was right—three months later, he and his wife got divorced.

Some time after that, he called her and suggested that they should catch up some time. Did she ever get back upstate? She was going to be there in two weeks, she replied. (She made that up on the spot.) He suggested dinner, and it was arranged. To paraphrase Molly, by the time the bread arrived, the restaurant could have gone up in smoke from the heat between the two of them. Now they were finally free to have the relationship that they should have had all along, and they saw each other long distance for three months.

Then she was diagnosed with skin cancer. Molly thought she should break things off: she didn't think it was fair to stick Seth with that kind of responsibility, so this time she disqualified herself. Or at least she tried. Seth wasn't having it at all. He'd learned from his previous mistake, and he wasn't letting her go. His response was to buy her a ring. Molly was treated and is doing just fine, but she wouldn't have been fine at all without Seth in her life.

Whew.

In all of these examples, fate intervened to throw couples back together, and we got the happy ending. I use them to illustrate just how close a call each of them was, and what all of these couples might have missed out on. But that's not how it generally works.

Far more often, self-disqualification does what it typically does, and a romance never happens.

Don't disqualify yourself. Give yourself a chance, and make sure your romance happens.

THOUGHT EXPERIMENT: Can you think of ways in which you might have disqualified yourself in the past? You know the sort of thing I mean:

- *"She's out of my league."*

- *"I saw the way he looked at her. What chance do I have?"*

- *"He's too _____ for me."*

- *"She's nice to me, but she's nice to everybody. There's no reason to believe she has any interest in me."*

Which ones have you used? And what might have happened had you not disqualified yourself? If you'd been rejected, how would your life be different? If you'd been accepted, how might your life be different?

IF AT FIRST YOU DON'T SUCCEED, TRY, TRY AGAIN. AND AGAIN. AND AGAIN.

In trying to make sense of our world, we love to learn by example. This can be very useful, but sometimes it can lead us in the wrong direction.

Most of us share a couple of unfortunate habits that regularly get in the way of our happiness. One of them is to judge decisions based on results. The other is to take a single example and generalize from it.

Let me explain what I mean. In the Super Bowl in 2015, the Seahawks attempted a pass at the end of the game, and it was intercepted, thus ending the game and costing them the championship. Most people thought they'd called the wrong play and should have run the ball instead. You've never heard such howling about what a terrible idea it was and what a moron the coach was.

The clamor was near unanimous, and it drowned out the voices of the statistical analysts, who upon cool reflection decided that the play call actually made a lot of sense. The result was the result, and for decades to come, die-hard football fans will be talking about how stupid the Seahawks were.

Let's visit an alternative reality: if the pass had been completed (which was entirely possible, except for a fantastic play by a New England defender), the play would have been hailed as daring and brilliant. If you don't know sports, trust me on this one. That's exactly how these things go.

We judge decisions based on results, and from this sample of one, sports fans have rendered their unshakeable judgment, even if it might be wrong. You don't want to make that same mistake in your love life.

If you're approaching your search for love in a healthy way, you shouldn't be deterred by a bad result. You might think you've found the right partner, only to get your heart broken. It might be bad luck, it might stem from a misunderstanding, or you might have fallen in with a skilled liar. Any number of things can happen through no fault of your own.

Or you might not meet anybody in the first place.

Neither of these results mean that you're doing anything wrong or that love can't possibly work for you. It took me 69 tries and three and a half years to meet Nancy. If I'd looked at the results from the first 68 and decided that it wasn't going to happen for me, I'd be alone right now, and very likely unhappy and frustrated.

Fortunately, I'd approached my search with a clear head, and for once my stubbornness served me. I thought I was on the right track, so I kept at it, and one day, there she was.

NO, SERIOUSLY, TRY AGAIN

Sometimes it's not simply about not getting the result you want. You might be one of the unfortunate many who have lived through a nightmarish relationship. That can be traumatic.

Both Nancy and I had extremely painful experiences in previous relationships, which I won't detail here out of respect for the privacy of those involved. As painful as our experiences were, there are plenty of people who have had it even worse than we did.

If you've had a traumatic experience in your love life, it is extremely easy to be gun shy. It is extremely easy to be mistrustful of entire genders.

You don't want to ever experience that sort of trauma again, and nobody can blame you.

The trick, then, is to remind yourself that not everyone is like your previous partner, and that love is possible. It's OK to be wary, though being too wary can be self-defeating.

Life does not provide us guarantees. It is filled with danger and people who sometimes do unspeakable things to each other. There's another end to that spectrum, however. If you're savvy enough and fortunate enough, you can avoid repeating those horrid experiences, and when you do, what's left is an amazing world, filled with wonder and opportunity.

With the right circumstances and the right partner, you have a legitimate chance to find the happiness you've longed for. If you've been burned, then by all means proceed with caution. But by all means proceed, so that your previous experiences don't ruin not only the times you've had, but the times you're going to have.

Nancy and I were fortunate enough to understand this, and even more fortunate to find each other. We gave ourselves that chance.

ONLINE DATING

If you don't have a job or go to school some place where there are lots and lots of single people, you might have a hard time meeting a large number of potential candidates for the love of your life. That's where online dating comes in: it's where the people are.

Let me be perfectly clear: online dating is not equally effective for everybody. Some people write better than others. Some people can't seem to take a good picture; others do. (When I had a friend who's a professional designer take a good picture of me, I immediately started getting more dates.) Some people seem to have all the right features for the search filters that people tend to apply, like education, height, income, and so on. Why wouldn't people pay attention to these things when they're searching? It's human nature, and besides, you have to use some basis for sifting through all of the profiles.

It was appalling to me to see how many 5'2" women were insisting on a guy 6'0" or taller. Seems like there must be a lot of terrific short guys who aren't getting as many dates as they should. If you're in the market for a great guy, you might want to search for the short ones! The same might hold true for tall women. People with decent incomes will also make it through the search filters, but those tell you nothing about net worth, debt, or fiscal responsibility.

It's important to note that the impressions you get online can be misleading. Peg, who we met earlier, thought she was looking for a male version of herself: she's a stage manager, kind of an artsy type, and she tends to dress and behave informally. So when Jason contacted her, she wasn't convinced that he'd be right for her. He's a lawyer, and that didn't fit with her expectations. His language was articulate, and, in the absence of his tone, his gestures, and his personality, she thought of him as being more formal and serious than she was. Maybe not a good fit. But she'd been learning, and gradually letting go of her expectations, so she agreed to meet him. He turned out to be terrific. After years of suspecting that there was nobody out there for her, she thought of Jason as "a nice rude awakening."

A lot of people are quick to imagine things that can go badly with online dating, but keep in mind that things can go badly with old-fashioned dates, too. Romance isn't easy, and it's not for the faint of heart. The fact is that although most people are pretty nice, some people are not nice at all, and that's life. Online dating can work really well. A third of all new marriages in the U.S. start online, according to a recent survey, and that number is likely growing.

One of those marriages was Carla's. Her literary agent told her the story of how she met her terrific husband on Match.com. The kicker was that the guy had been living right around the corner from her. But physical proximity wasn't enough for them: they still weren't able to meet the old-fashioned way, and going online was what brought them together. Once they got together, the sparks flew.

Thus inspired, Carla resolved to run home and get on Match. She didn't do it immediately, though: she was already on eHarmony and wanted to make sure she was doing the right thing before she started paying for another service. She wrote in her day planner that if eHarmony hadn't worked by January 2, she was going to sign up for Match. In fact she did meet someone on eHarmony, but after a very promising start, he vanished without a trace.

She was bothered, she was depressed, and she was suddenly motivated to move up her timetable and sign up on December 16. Eleven days later, she was presented with Curtis's profile. She wrote to him, and they started a little correspondence. On January 2nd, the date she'd resolved to get started, Curtis asked her out for a lunch date. Had he not met her, Curtis was going to let his profile expire at the end of the year. January 2 would have been too late.

They hit it off in a big way and had a ton of things in common, which made them feel like they understood each other in ways that nobody else could. When Carla described him to her brother, he said "So you fell in love with yourself." She gushed about Curtis to her friends, and in her own turn inspired them to sign up. Both of her girlfriends have now been with their new guys for a year. At her wedding, the photographer told her that most of the couples he'd photographed lately had met on Match.

I recommend the online method to my dating clients for a simple reason: it's where the single people are. You will find far more possibilities with online dating than without it. Now, there's certainly no guarantee that you'll actually get dates with these people, but you'll know where they are, and the system gives you a chance to connect.

You can jump into the deep end of the online pool, or just dip a toe in. You might just toss a profile out there and see if anybody writes you. That's not the best way to do it, but it gives you a chance that you don't have if you don't do anything at all.

You might make a point of contacting a certain number of people each week, or each month. Some people will always get more hits than others, but that's OK. If traffic is slow, maybe you can work on a better profile. Maybe you don't fare well on the online search filters, like age, weight, height, or income. Maybe you need a better photograph. And maybe you won't get much traffic regardless of what you do. You can feel bad about that, or you can budget for it, and keep giving yourself a chance. If nobody writes to you, you can write to them. But maybe you'll do better than you think you will.

Understand that there is someone out there who can appreciate you for the special things that are so right about you. You have to be patient and diligent and find them. Just like Tatum the librarian did, earlier in this book. You could write to some of those people you find online, to see if they're among the rare ones. You don't have to invite them for coffee—you can just start up a conversation. Whatever feels right. It's OK to be daring, OK to be spontaneous, OK to create your own luck.

Ideas for a better profile:

- *Put up a few dynamite photos of yourself.* Even if you're not particularly photogenic, you can make the best of it. You can hire a professional or pick the best out of a hundred shots that friend takes of you. Whatever works.

- *Put up a flattering head shot*, preferably with your best smile.

- *If you think a shot that shows off your physique will help you, by all means use one.* It doesn't have to reveal too much to get the job done.

- *Say something about yourself that acts as a teaser:* something that makes you interesting but doesn't disqualify you.

- *Avoid clichés.* When I was dating online, woman after woman would say that they cleaned up nicely or that they looked equally good in jeans or a cocktail dress. This didn't make them seem unique in any way.

- *Scout the competition:* you can go onto a dating website and see what others are saying about themselves. You can steal an idea, or you can separate yourself with something fresh and interesting that other people aren't saying.

If you're not being inundated with requests to go out, you should consider expanding your search. Keep in mind one simple principle: you can say no. Most people online are used to it. Rejection is always difficult, but it's easier when you've never met someone, and it's part of the deal, like it or not. So don't be afraid to cast a wide net and then throw a bunch back.

Here are some ideas for finding more interesting candidates:

Expand the age range you'd consider.	Someone a bit older might still be attractive. Someone a bit younger might be mature and interesting. You don't have to date them, but it does no harm to look.
Expand the range of heights you'd consider.	If they're fantastic in every other way, height doesn't have to matter. You might be surprised how quickly you get used to somebody taller or shorter than you had in mind.
Expand the distance that they live from you.	Even if a given distance is daunting for you, it might not seem so far if you fall in love. And maybe your candidate doesn't mind traveling, or comes your way often anyway. If either you or your candidate has the money to travel, even a long distance isn't always a deal-breaker. I once had a long distance relationship (separate states) that might have worked if our personalities meshed better, and I still got a great friendship out of the deal.
Consider other races.	If you think you're attracted to one racial type, it doesn't hurt to surprise yourself. Step outside your comfort zone, and you might find someone who suits you wonderfully, at which point they'll become attractive very quickly.
Consider other religious points of view.	If two people have great rapport and respect each other's differences, a great deal is possible.

Consider different educational levels.	There are plenty of incredibly smart people who didn't get too far in school, and plenty of people with advanced degrees who are simple, down-to-earth types. What matters is mutual respect and rapport.
Consider different income levels.	Someone without money can be very responsible and might add all sorts of other things to your life. And income isn't the same as wealth, so they might have more money than you think. Conversely, if you're afraid that your lack of money or a financial disparity might create problems from their perspective, there's no harm in finding out.

There are many ways that you can expand your search, whether online or offline. The important thing to remember is that the more people you correspond with and potentially meet with, the better your chances are of finding someone terrific. If you're exhausted by the thought of all of those messages or coffee dates, you can do things at your own rate while still keeping that principle in mind. And remember that when you keep things in perspective and take the pressure off of any given encounter, you can meet a relatively large number of people with a relatively modest emotional investment.

DATING APPS

Dating apps are essentially another way of using technology to meet people you wouldn't otherwise meet. Tinder allows you to see and quickly swipe yes or no on potential matches in your area or even your immediate vicinity in real time. Grindr is similar but geared toward the LGBT community. Hinge adds in the comfort factor of mutual friends.

You can use whichever might work for you, if any. New apps will be cropping up all the time, and by the time this book is published, one or two of those apps might already be falling out of favor and losing value as a way to meet people

So there isn't one right app to use, any more than there is one online dating service. They're all just opportunities. Opportunities to meet someone terrific.

Consider whether any of them fit your style, consider the upside and the downside, and judge for yourself whether this app or that is going to help you find somebody. Work the problem, and use the tools at your disposal to give yourself your best chance at happiness.

SOCIAL MEDIA

If you're not excited about going out, you can still connect. Online dating is one way, but there are others. Social media is a great way to maintain old friendships and to foster more recent ones. Sometimes you can even create new friendships with someone you've never met in person; you can sometimes get to know someone a little through a conversation with a mutual friend. And there's a comfort level in knowing that they are liked and trusted by someone you like and trust.

While James was going to school at Alfred University in upstate New York, he visited a friend at Cornell. The friend had a roommate, and the roommate had a friend: Tasha. There was an immediate click, and Tasha thought James would make a great friend. She suggested that they exchange contact information, and they stayed in touch. James was interested in the romantic possibilities, but despite the click, Tasha wasn't there yet: she didn't want to commit to anything while she was still in school. As they communicated back and forth, she was by her own admission "kind of mean to him." As I spoke with them, James said "you thought you were being mean," and though they argued semantics, it was clear that he maintained an interest. But with nothing happening in the moment, their communications became less frequent, and after a while they weren't in touch more often than once or twice a year.

Through a group conversation on Facebook, they realized that they both had dogs about the same age, named Maya and Misha. The dogs were all they needed to really get talking again. They talked, and talked some more.

Only now the equation had changed: they both lived in New York, he in Brooklyn and she in the Bronx. Tasha had just finished graduate school and had more free time than she'd had in years. So when in the course of things James asked her out, it suddenly seemed like a very good idea.

He took the three-hour convoluted commute from one end of New York to the other, and the rest of their romance went the old-fashioned way: dinner and a movie, flowers on Valentine's Day, and now an engagement. All of that sounds easy enough, but it might never have happened without Facebook providing a convenient, pressure-free way to reestablish a connection.

THE NEXT TECHNOLOGY

There's online dating, there's social media, there are phone apps…
it doesn't much matter what the next technology is. All of them
have advantages and drawbacks, and most of them will have
some sort of learning curve. All of them are tools, and if used
judiciously, they might improve your chances of finding love.

Don't worry about the details of the next big thing—worry about
the principles set forth in this book and apply them to whatever
it is. Figure out what means are available. If you're not sure, ask
around and make the best of whatever you have to work with.

A thoughtful approach and a healthy outlook are more important
than any silver-bullet technology that might come along.

CHAPTER 5
IT WORKED! NOW WHAT?

OK. You've gotten the message about being yourself, you've expanded your world with the people around you, and hey! It worked! You have a terrific partner.

Now don't mess it up.

Maintaining a relationship is just as important as finding one, if you want that satisfying life you're always daydreaming about. Making a relationship work is a huge topic for another book entirely, but here are a few quick reminders of some things you should probably be doing to make sure that this great new relationship stays great:

- *Work on yourself, not your partner.* People can and do change, but not because you told them to. You can change, though, and you can always work on making yourself a better partner.

- *Put on their shoes.* Any time there's a difference of opinion, it's a good idea to try to really understand where the other person is coming from. Even if you don't ultimately agree, it's important to at least let their side of the story be heard.

- *You're responsible for your happiness.* People sometimes tend to view their partner as responsible for their happiness, but they're not. You are. Your partner is not your employee.

- *Build trust, earn respect.* You can't insist that someone trust you or respect you. Those things will flow naturally out of your actions, if your actions warrant them.

- *Play like a team.* When you have trust or respect, you can start playing like a team. Both of you can think about things that improve your relationship and your collective happiness. It's not a competition to see who can squeeze the most out of the other. Paradoxically, you'll get more out of the other when you start demanding less and giving more, because if you've got a good partner, they'll naturally be motivated to give more in return.

- *Communicate.* Your partner isn't clairvoyant. Let them know what's on your mind. Listen to them and pay attention to their actions even if they're not saying anything.

- *Communicate well.* Talk candidly and regularly, in a kind and respectful manner. Make the discussion about the issue and not about the person. Pay attention to your tone of voice. Foster good communication by listening, and don't punish your partner for telling the truth. If you are kind and patient, your partner will want to communicate.

- *Ask, don't tell.* Words matter. Again, your partner isn't your employee. Ask for the things you want; don't issue orders. Be prepared: if you ask for something and they say no, you can either accept it or you can explain why it's important to you. Most of the time, a good partner will either want to comply or will offer a clear, justifiable reason why they shouldn't.

- *Commit to trying.* Don't expect a perfect relationship, and don't imagine that a good relationship comes for free.

Assume that you're going to have to work at it, and commit to doing the best you can to help it succeed. A great relationship is worth making a real effort for.

CHAPTER 6

LOOKING IN THE LAST PLACE—THE SHORT FORM

So to review, here are the broad strokes of what you need to do to find love while doing it your way:

- *Understand **WHY** you want to find love:*
    - Be clear about the fact that having a great partner is your best path to a lifetime of happiness. Commit yourself to going out and finding that person, diligently and with a consistent, sustainable effort. Prepare yourself for it to take time, and prepare yourself for a bumpy ride along the way.

- *Understand **WHAT** you're doing:*
    - Forget your long list of superficial requirements. Focus on finding a really good human being with whom you have terrific rapport, and watch love grow.

- *Understand **HOW** you're going to do it:*
    - Let a great connection determine who your partner will be; don't pursue an attractive person and force a connection that isn't genuine.
    - Don't worry about the big date. Connect with people any way you can, without caring about how

exactly you meet them, what you're doing, or what the end result will be. You'll find your partner in the last place you look.

- Try to do things you enjoy as you're trying to connect. That helps you live your life the way you want, and it encourages you to get out and connect some more. Be as happy as you can, regardless of the outcome of your search.

- Once you've made the connection, make it work, through kindness, understanding, communication, and love.

Repeat as necessary until you've got your keeper. Live happily ever after.

ACKNOWLEDGEMENTS

I'm embarrassed to confess that it took me a few decades to figure out just how important it is to ask other people for help, but I'm proud to say that I've absolutely got the hang of it now. I received a huge amount of help in making this book happen.

I'd like to start by profusely thanking whichever deserving person I might have left out of these acknowledgements. I'm certain of your existence, and I owe you dinner.

I'd like to thank Jennifer Jacobson and Jane Kurtz for early encouragement. Enormous gratitude is due the fabulous Alison James for all sorts of crucial contributions to this book. I'd like to thank my great pal Edie Freedman for her expert eye and her huge help in putting the manuscript together. I'd like to thank the indefatigable spirit that is Juli Greenwood for her can-do and her know-how in helping me to get the word out. I'd like to thank my many readers, including but not limited to Amy Conklin, Jacqueline Davies, Michelle Hewitt, A.M. Jenkins, Kate Jovin, Dian Curtis Regan, Amy Butler Greenfield, and Melissa Wyatt, for their efforts and their insights.

Of course I must thank my beloved wife, Nancy Werlin, to whom this book is dedicated. She not only stars in the narrative, but she made me believe this book was possible, supported me with her extensive wisdom about the publishing process, and did the whole wind-beneath-my-wings routine. I can't overstate her importance to this effort, in ways both big and small.

Lastly, this book wouldn't be possible without the many, many women and men who generously related to me their own dating experiences, and provided me with much of my material. You know who you are, and you made all the difference.

ABOUT THE AUTHOR

Jim McCoy is an award-winning life coach who dated for three years at mid-life. He now lives outside Boston with his wife, *New York Times* bestselling YA author Nancy Werlin. You can reach Jim through his website at www.merlincoaching.com or on Facebook at Merlin Coaching.